Praise for
Think Like Tiger

"The book makes clear how Tiger outthinks all of his competitors and is full of common-sense advice about how amateurs can do the same."   —*The Baltimore Sun*

"John Andrisani is one of the most prolific authors of golf articles and books on the face of this planet . . . [and] *Think Like Tiger* may very well be what you need to take your game to another and higher level."   —*Golf Today* magazine

THINK LIKE TIGER

An Analysis of Tiger Woods'
Mental Game

by John Andrisani

A PERIGEE BOOK

A Perigee Book
Published by The Berkley Publishing Group
A division of Penguin Putnam Inc.
375 Hudson Street
New York, NY 10014

G. P. Putnam's Sons hardcover edition: April 2002
First Perigee trade paperback edition: April 2003

Perigee trade paperback edition ISBN: 0-399-52860-1

Visit our website at www.penguinputnam.com

The Library of Congress has catalogued the
G. P. Putnam's Sons edition as follows:

Andrisani, John.
Think like Tiger : an analysis of Tiger Woods'
mental game / by John Andrisani.
p. cm.
Includes index.
ISBN 0-399-14843-4
1. Golf—Psychological aspects. 2. Woods, Tiger. I. Title.
GV979.P75A55   2002   2001048900
796.352'01'9—dc21

Printed in the United States of America

10 9 8 7 6 5 4 3 2 1

I dedicate this book to Tiger's mother, Kultida (Tida); and father, Earl; clinical psychologist Dr. Jay Brunza; and teachers Rudy Duran, John Anselmo, and Claude "Butch" Harmon, Jr., for enlightening Tiger Woods and teaching him the value of the mind-body-spirit link to good golf.

The general who wins a battle makes many calculations
in his temple before the battle is fought.

SUN TZU, *The Art of War*

CONTENTS

FOREWORD

I TAUGHT TIGER WOODS FROM THE AGE OF TEN until eighteen and played with him around twenty-five times, so I think I'm qualified to comment on why he is such a special golfer.

Physically, Tiger's flexibility stands out as a most prominent asset and is a vital link to an exceptionally powerful swing. And understandably so, because Tiger works hard stretching his muscles. As well, Tiger has superior feel in his hands and great eye focus necessary for judging distances of shots.

Mentally, Tiger's focus while competing under extreme pressure is uncanny. When Tiger stands over a shot preparing to swing and stares at the target, there's a cool and calculating look in his eyes. When you look at him, you just know he's visualizing the ball flying toward the target. And once he makes that controlled high-speed swing and hits the ball, his tee shots frequently finish in the middle of the fairway and his approach shots near—or in—the hole.

Tiger was not just blessed at birth; he had a first-rate team of skilled individuals behind him, a "think tank" to help him improve at a very rapid rate.

I'm honored to say I was one of the official members of "Team Tiger," and just how I helped Tiger become a better player is documented in *A-Game Golf,* a book John Andrisani wrote with me and one that concentrates more on the physical side of golf than the mental. This latest book of Andrisani's, on the other hand, contains a great deal of insightful information about the mental game of Tiger's, and golfing legends, too, plus it reveals how I, and others, played a role in Tiger's development.

Rudy Duran, who preceded me as Tiger's golf instructor, also deserves credit. So does Dr. Jay Brunza, a clinical psychologist who used some unique mental training techniques to teach Tiger how to enter the "zone" and generally use his head to think more intelligently on the course.

As much as Duran, Brunza, and I did to help Tiger, his parents, Earl and Tida, did more, especially with respect to the mental side of golf. Earl taught Tiger the fundamentals of logical course management; namely, how to get the ball around the course without making unforced mental errors. He also taught Tiger how to be mentally tough—to play his own game and stay on his preplanned success path, instead of letting himself be distracted by the shots, scores, or gamesmanship of other golfers.

Tida taught Tiger to be mentally patient and tenacious on the golf course and, most of all, to concentrate intently. When interviewing Tida on behalf of John Andrisani, even I was surprised to hear that she started taking Tiger to a Buddhist temple when he was young so that he could learn how to enhance his mind-control skills through deep meditation.

All these discoveries and secrets of Tiger's success make this book an interesting read and, more important, a guidebook for improvement. For starters, you will learn to make the mental side of golf a priority. You will also learn the art of making the mind-body-spirit connection. Additionally, you will learn how to play to your potential, by applying the thinking process to your setup, swing, and shot-making game. After all, as Tiger knows only too well, you can have the best swing technique in the world, but if you don't know how to make the brain matter in between your ears work for you, you will fail to shoot the low scores you are capable of shooting. This book will show you how to lower your scores by using your head on the golf course. In fact,

Andrisani even includes mental buzz phrases to help you solve some classic swing and shot-making problems.

Good luck in your journey, which will involve delving into your mind and exploring the true spirit of the game of golf—mental frontiers that all great golfers throughout history have learned to tap into.

JOHN ANSELMO
Huntington Beach, California

INTRODUCTION

SINCE GOLF WAS FIRST PLAYED NEARLY SIX HUNDRED years ago on the links of St. Andrews in Scotland, thousands of instructional books have been written, mostly by professional teachers and tour players but occasionally by amateurs, too—most notably, Bobby Jones. All but a few of these texts deal only with the physical side of golf: how to set up correctly to the ball, employ a smooth, technically sound backswing, and swing down powerfully through impact into a full finish position.

It's ironic that, regardless of the high number of instruction books sold and the availability of sophisticated equipment and expert teachers employed by country clubs across the country, the majority of recreational golfers still shoot high scores. Only a small percentage of golfers play to single-figure handicaps, and fewer still shoot par scores on a regular basis. Why?

In answering this question, I think it most appropriate to quote Arnold Haultain, one of the forefathers of mind golf and author of the book *The Mystery of Golf,* first published in 1908, then reprinted two years later because of its popularity, then once again in 1986 for the same reason.

To play golf well a man must play like a machine; but like a machine in which the mental-motor must be perfect as the muscular mechanism.

Precise coordination of hand and eye is necessary; this coordination is directed by nerve currents (cerebral and cerebro-spinal) conveyed to the muscles. Unless the supreme and regulatory centers of intelligence, wherein lie embedded the cells from which orders for muscular movement derive, are first, in thorough working order, and, second, intent upon the business at hand, the order conveyed through the delicate muscular fibers of the fingers, hands, wrists, legs, and arms will be ineffectual, and the resulting stroke inaccurate.

Although these and other statements made by Haultain are true, he offers no practical solutions for improving one's swing through mind exercises and fails to explain the full magnitude of the mental side of golf. Still, because he introduced golfers to the mind-body connection relative to the swing and encouraged others to explore the psychological aspects of golf, his book remains a classic.

One such mind explorer was Michael Murphy, whose best-selling book *Golf in the Kingdom* (1972) examines the spiritual side of golf. Yet, it too offers few specific ways for golfers to improve. Like *The Mystery of Golf,* however, Murphy's book proved to be a step in the right direction and a further incentive to others to keep exploring the mind for answers about how to swing and score better.

Three of the most impressive books to date dealing with the mind's role in golf are *The Inner Game of Golf* (1981) by Timothy Gallwey, *Golfing in the Zone* (1996) by Larry Miller, and *Mental Management for Great Golf* (1996) by Dr. Bee Epstein-Shepherd. The first two books are more spiritually orientated yet do guide golfers along a path of practical improvement, made possible by transcending existing swing principles and adopting instead psychological principles that allow one's subconscious to take control. For example, Gallwey helped a golfer cure a slice by instructing him to stop trying so hard to think about the so-called evergreen basics for swinging the club that he'd memorized and practiced over and over. The student was told "not to try to see what happens." As a result, he let go of inhibitions, employed a natural flowing swing, and hit accurate shots.

Miller, in similar fashion, was able to get an elderly man to hit the ball more powerfully and accurately by having him forget about obsessing about the technical points of the swing and instead concentrating on making the swinging club create a loud swish sound in the hitting area.

Both Gallwey and Miller allow the golfer to enter a new dimension and improve his or her swing in very unorthodox ways, yet I would have preferred that they had delved more deeply into how using one's head on the course can promote lower scores.

Epstein-Shepherd, by presenting keys to keen shotmaking visualization and confidence and concentration enhancement, helps golfers appreciate the mental side of golf as a vital link to lasting good play. Still, her intelligent instruction falls short when it comes to relating the mind to the total scope of the game.

In *Think Like Tiger,* I analyze the total game of golf's greatest player, Tiger Woods, and reveal how he evolved into a supreme on-course thinker. In the history of golf, there has never been a better swinger and shotmaker than Tiger Woods. PGA Tour players, golf press, tournament promoters, and the golfing public all know that's a fact. However, what so many golfers around the world fail to realize is that Tiger's phenomenal mental game is what fuels the fire and, further, that this is an asset of his game he was *not* born with. Like the forming of a diamond, it took time to develop. Like the making of a fine wine, it relied on the care of others.

It's Tiger's mental supremacy that allows him to:

1. stay confident from the start of the round to its finish
2. remain in a cocoon of concentration when preparing to hit a shot
3. pick the right club a high percentage of the time
4. set up square to the ball over and over
5. focus intently on the target and stay focused under pressure
6. consistently picture, then repeat, a rhythmic and powerful swing
7. hit spectacular on-target shots in almost every tournament he competes in
8. stay in control of his emotions most of the time throughout the round
9. learn from his mistakes. As good as Tiger is, he realizes what sports psychologist Dr. Bob Rotella preaches: "Golf is not a game of perfect." Consequently, he knows how to keep himself in the game mentally after hitting a bad shot, getting a bad bounce, making the wrong choice of club or shot, or watching an opponent hit a miracle shot.
10. dominate the world of professional golf

Tiger learned a lot about the swing by mentally visualizing his father's action, then mimicking it. However, whereas other parents are happy to see their son or daughter hit solid shots, Earl and Tida Woods were not satisfied and encouraged Tiger to work beyond the shot. Earl taught Tiger to think about various shot-making options before swinging—the essence of good course management—when taking him out for playing lessons. He also taught him to become mentally tough by forcing him to withstand distractions. Tida taught Tiger the importance of patience, tenacity, and perseverance, both in life and on the golf course, plus the value of meditation. Rich Learner of The Golf Channel says that "when Tiger was young and hit bad shots, his Buddhist mother reminded him that he was human, capable of making mistakes. The secret, as she explained, was not to make the same mistake twice and channel any anger into positive energy to make future shots better."

To help Tiger become a better, more rounded player, his father arranged for him to take lessons from two California-based teachers: Rudy Duran and John Anselmo. Duran taught Tiger from the age of five until ten. At that point, Anselmo took over and taught Tiger until he was eighteen. Together, these two teachers helped Tiger hone a top-notch setup, swing, and shot-making game by learning to make mind-body connections and shoot lower scores by using his head to play high-percentage shots.

Butch Harmon took over where Anselmo left off, taking Tiger to the next level by teaching him mind-game se-crets he learned from his dad, Claude Harmon, Sr., winner of the 1948 Masters, and other great players such as Ben Hogan and Jack Burke, Jr.

For a large part of Tiger's amateur life, one other man played a major role in his development: Dr. Jay Brunza, a Navy clinical psychologist who taught Tiger the secrets to playing in the "zone" during a round of golf. Tiger's mother was so proud of Brunza and all the individuals who helped Tiger in his formative years that she had "Team Tiger" T-shirts made.

In *Think Like Tiger,* I don't purport to be able to read Tiger Woods' mind. I analyze Tiger's mental game in the same in-depth manner I analyzed his power-driving game in the book *The Tiger Woods Way,* and his pitching, chip-ping, bunker play, and putting techniques in *The Short Game Magic of Tiger Woods*. Furthermore, my information is based on my own expertise as a former golf instructor and senior instruction editor at *Golf* magazine. To further enhance the mental-game message, I offer insights garnered from Tiger's family, friends, fellow competitors, former caddy, former personal psychologist, and former teachers. Addi-tionally, I rely on information from other top golf instruc-tors, sports psychologists, and respected golf journalists.

I'm very proud to say that I'm the first golf writer to fully explore the mind and its expansive application to golf, using such a masterful player as Tiger Woods as the ultimate role model. From the time you start reading *Think Like Tiger,* you will learn once and for all the truth behind the golf cliché "Golf is 99 percent mental." You will learn how to take control of your game by developing a new on-course program, one that allows you to trust your swing and think your way to lower scores.

No matter what your handicap is, if you're looking to shave strokes off your score without totally revamping your present swing, let *Think Like Tiger* be your new guidebook to lasting improvement. Enjoy the mind trip.

JOHN ANDRISANI
Sarasota, Florida

1.

THE THINK TANK

Good advice from his parents, top teachers, and a
prominent psychologist, plus learning from
legendary professional golfers, educated
Tiger on the value of mind control.

NOWADAYS, AN INCREASING NUMBER OF TOP
PGA Tour and LPGA golf professionals improve
their swings and scores by working closely with sports psychologists. In turn, these mind coaches pass along their secrets to golfers through such vehicles as the Golf Channel
and *Golf* magazine. Consequently, more and more country
club players are beginning to realize the vital role the mind
plays in promoting a technically sound golf swing, powerfully hit drives, strategically placed approach shots, pinpoint pitches, accurate chips, on-target bunker shots, and
on-line putts.

Mental gurus, most notably Dr. Bob Rotella, work regularly with big-name pros and prove day in and day out that golf *is* 99 percent mental. What goes on between the ears during an eighteen-hole round has a big influence on how we deal with course situations and direct the golf ball toward the hole. And many top golf instructors such as Jim Flick, who has coached Jack Nicklaus, one of the game's premier thinkers, are bringing home that point. "The game of golf begins in your mind, more than athletic ability, more than technique, more than practice or equipment or anything else. The mind-set or attitude you bring to the game determines not only the enjoyment you desire from golf but also the level of proficiency you will achieve," said Flick in his book, *Jim Flick on Golf.*

Mind control is the only true shortcut to playing to your potential. No pro knows this fact better than Tiger Woods, golf's genius who thrives on pressure, because very early on in his life he was taught by the people around him how to think his way to lower scores. Additionally, Tiger was positively influenced by the examples of golfing legends who during their heyday used their minds to make their bodies swing the club correctly and hit excellent golf shots consistently.

TIGER'S EARLY MENTAL TRAINING
FROM EARL WOODS

Tiger's mind-golf home-schooling program began when he was just a toddler watching his father, Earl, hit shots into a net set up in the garage of the family's California home. Earl was smart to leave Tiger strapped in his high chair rather than letting him hold a golf club right away and develop bad swing habits because he did not have a clue about how to swing.

According to Earl, Tiger's first teacher and author of *Training a Tiger,* the longer Tiger watched, the more he learned the elements of a good golf swing through the process of assimilation. Each time Earl swung the club, new data were obviously fed into Tiger's brain, speeding up the learning process. Tiger seemingly felt each and every action via visual transmission—especially the club-to-ball hit as he looked down from his perched position. This kind of training, which centered on the student mentally rehearsing the physical actions involved in the swing, is very similar to what Olympic sharpshooters do before a competition. They work on dry-run shooting, making believe they are holding a gun, looking through a scope, getting the target in the crosshairs, and finally pulling the trigger. That way, when it actually comes time to hold the rifle and shoot at a target during competition, they feel more confident and usually perform the physical action to near perfection. Which is exactly what Tiger did, when, at ten months old, he jumped down from his high chair and started swinging like his father. Still, you can have the best swinging action in the world, but if your body and club are not aligned correctly at address and you fail to visualize a good shot in your mind before you swing, the ball is far less likely to fly toward its intended target.

Understanding this profound statement, together with further advice given to Tiger by his father about the value of setting up correctly and seeing the perfect shot come to life in the mind's eye, had a positive effect on Tiger. Throughout his amateur career and now, as a pro, he takes great care when preparing to play a shot.

Watch Tiger play on television or live at a tournament and you'll notice immediately, from the gaze in his eyes, how he enters a trance when preparing to hit a shot. When first standing behind the ball, then jockeying his feet and body into the correct setup position, then next setting the club down on the grass behind the ball, he stares at the target intently. It's obvious from Tiger's actions that he knows what every other top-quality golfer knows:

1. A good setup means a square setup, and you arrive in this basic starting position by setting the clubface down perpendicular to the ball and target and setting your body parallel to an imaginary target line. The target line extends from the ball to the target.

2. The setup, to a large degree, determines the type of swing you make.

3. Eyeing the target takes your mind off swinging at the ball and allows you to concentrate on swinging the club through it.

Tiger was fortunate to be the son of low-handicap player who paid such close attention to the setup. Many parents make the mistake of letting their children hit balls right away and develop bad habits, unlike Tiger's father. For Tiger's benefit, Earl constantly demonstrated the square-address position, apparently knowing that children like to learn through imitation. He also showed Tiger how to position the hands parallel to each other (with the back of the left hand square to the clubface), flex the knees a little, bend forward slightly from the waist, and relax the arms. Additionally, he showed Tiger the basic movements of the swing, most notably the parallel position of the backswing (clubshaft parallel to the target line at the top), and a balanced finish position. Whenever possible, Earl used mental imagery to help convey the most important physical elements of the swing. For example, when showing Tiger how the shoulders and hips should turn clockwise on the backswing then counterclockwise on the downswing, he told him to imagine a door opening and closing.

While Earl showed Tiger the vital positions of the setup and swing, Tiger watched attentively, all the time building a clear picture in his mind of what was correct. This one-on-one instruction allowed Tiger to store a wealth of golf knowledge in his brain. According to his past and present coaches, he still draws on that data bank today, proving that the basics of the setup and swing are evergreen.

Up until the time Tiger turned four, his father covered a lot of ground as his sole teacher. In addition to teaching Tiger the basics of the preshot routine, namely eyeing the target, the elements of the setup, and the most important points of the swing, Earl instructed him on the total game, all the time making a *mental connection*. For example, when teaching Tiger how to pitch the ball, he stressed the importance of concentrating on the conditions of lie, pin position, firmness of the green, wind, and the position of hazards, to help him determine whether to hit a high, floating pitch shot or a low, knockdown pitch. He also wanted Tiger to note mentally how far he hit the ball in the air with different-length, different-speed swings.

When chipping, Tiger was taught to focus on a landing spot on the edge of the green and hone in on the ball and target to get a feel for distance.

When hitting bunker shots, Earl instructed Tiger to zero in on a spot about three inches behind the ball and concentrate on contacting that spot with the club at impact.

When putting, Earl wanted Tiger to imagine the ball falling into the hole before he employed a stroke.

When Tiger practiced the full swing on the driving

range, Earl made sure that he was aiming at a target, not just hitting shots into the open field as many amateur golfers do.

Earl's swing tips certainly allowed Tiger to do some amazing things as a young boy, like looking like a pro hitting a golf ball into a net, at age three, on *The Mike Douglas Show*. All the same, when I asked Earl to put down in writing the two most important things he taught Tiger, his written response was "course management and mental toughness." Now, a less experienced golfer would not be so impressed, asking, "That's *all* Earl taught Tiger?" However, any good golfer knows what I mean when I say those few words cover a heck of a lot of territory.

As soon as Tiger first hit the links of the Navy Golf Course at age two, his father explained to him that swinging well and hitting solid shots was one thing and scoring was another. To score well, you have to play with your head and not your heart. You must use common sense when hitting shots from tee to green and know what are "green-light," "yellow-light," and "red-light" course situations. Being a good golfer himself, Earl enlightened Tiger, spelling out the differences between these strategies.

A green-light situation means the percentages are in your favor and you can go on the attack, knowing the risk is worth the reward.

A yellow-light situation means just what it means on the road: Proceed with caution. For example, if the hole is situated on the right side of a green, with a lake to the right, you should play a safe shot by hitting the ball left of the hole, to the "fat," or wide, area of the green.

A red-light situation simply calls for you to stop what you are doing, or intending to do, and regroup. For example, if on a par-four hole, you face a second shot of two hundred and thirty-five yards over water to the green, and that's the longest distance you have ever hit a three-wood, stop! Put the three-wood back in your bag, take out an iron, then hit a layup shot short of the water. You can always pitch the ball close and make the putt for a hard-earned par.

In educating Tiger, Earl taught him to start thinking about his next shot practically the split second he hit the ball. When you're this conscientious, you feel more confident mentally. However, to be superconfident, like Tiger, you have to know how to manage your golf game in other course situations.

Off the tee, on a curving "dogleg" par four or par five, it's advantageous to hit the ball down the side of the fairway that offers the best angle to hit an approach shot into the green. Sometimes, it's best not to hit a driver on a dogleg left or right hole, to avoid hitting the ball through the fairway into the woods or deep rough. Sometimes, too, it's smarter to use a long iron or three-wood off the tee of a straight par-four or par-five hole. This is especially true if the hole is very narrow. However, this rule of thumb still applies if there's a chance you could drive the ball far enough to reach a cross bunker or water hazard or land the ball on a steep downhill slope in the fairway that is bound to play havoc with your approach into the green.

Tiger and other intelligent players also often play a left-to-right fade or right-to-left draw off the tee. They hit either of these type shots to work the ball away from lurking hazards and back to the center of the fairway or to effectively shorten the hole by turning the ball around the corner of the dogleg. Players who choose to draw the ball smartly tee up on the left side of the tee box and hit away from trouble, while those who prefer to hit a fade tee up on the right side. (I'll review what I believe are Tiger's mental and physical keys for playing fade and draw shots in chapter 5.)

On par-three holes, you must also think before you act, as Tiger does. Before you pick a club, be sure to calculate the correct yardage to the hole, and determine the strength and direction of the wind. Pros and low-handicap golfers play a stronger club for every ten miles per hour of headwind (i.e., a five iron instead of a six iron) and choose a weaker club when playing a shot downwind (i.e., a six iron instead of a five iron). Experienced players also take into consideration any slopes that could affect the way the ball bounces and rolls once it lands. The last thing you want to happen is to hit a seven iron, say one hundred and fifty yards, and have the ball hit a downhill slope in front of the hole, then bounce over the green.

Good course managers also realize the importance of

not being influenced by the clubs used by fellow medal-play competitors, match-play opponents, or playing partners in a weekend Nassau game.

Many high-handicap players make the mistake of using a medium iron on a relatively long par-three hole just because another player in their foursome did, when they know a long iron or a utility wood is the right play. Choose the club that will allow you to reach the hole, while making a smooth swing. Taking less club, for fear of embarrassment, or due to a big ego, is anything but a smart strategy.

In hitting any length approach shot, you should also use your head. Tiger is so savvy that he figures out what side of the green is best to miss on should the shot not come off, and this affects the type of shot he initially hits. For example, if there's a water hazard left of the putting green and only manicured fringe grass right, he'll play a draw to avoid the hazard. If the shot comes off, he's putting for birdie. If not, he can still save par with a chip and a putt. It's this kind of supersmart thinking that prompts fellow PGA Tour player Chris Di Marco to say: "Tiger thinks his way around the course better than any other player."

Tiger really uses his head on and around the greens, as you should, because there's less margin for error. When playing a short- to medium-length putt that breaks only slightly, concentrate on making a firmer stroke, so in essence you take the break out, and bang the ball into an imaginary miniature target in the back of the cup.

When preparing to hit a long putt, especially one downhill on a very fast green, you should analyze the break from all sides of the hole. You should also imagine a two-foot circle around the hole, then lag the ball up into your round target area to ensure a two putt, rather than charge the cup and risk three putting. This mental trick, taught to Tiger by his father, will help alleviate anxiety when you are competing and help you manage your game better in a pressure-filled match.

On breaking putts, an intelligent strategy is to point the logo, printed on the ball, in the direction you want the ball to first start rolling, before it curves or breaks. Making this part of your putting routine will make you more confident about holing out.

"Earl Woods was an extra-special mentor of Tiger's," says Julius Richardson, the United States Golf Teachers Federation 2000 Teacher of the Century, who is also on *Golf* magazine's 2001 list of the 100 Best Teachers in America. "One evening, in Chicago, I had dinner with Earl and I asked him what he did most to help Tiger with course management. Earl told me that when he played with Tiger, he'd let him make a strategic mistake, such as taking a silly, low-percentage risk in hitting a shot over water. Then, a moment later, he would correct Tiger on the spot while the course error was fresh in his mind. It was this type of early training that helped Tiger minimize mental errors on the golf course, such as not taking enough time to concentrate and read a lie properly, and selecting the wrong club as a result. Earl's lessons have really paid off, since Tiger can never be accused of giving a tournament away due to making unforced errors."

THE OTHER MENTAL TIPS GIVEN TO TIGER BY EARL were much more serious and designed to toughen him up and prepare him to do battle with "dirty" opponents. These type of golfers representing the ugly side of golf believe that gamesmanship is part of the game and like to win at all costs. Therefore, you must be prepared.

To mentally prepare Tiger to play "extreme golf," Earl purposely distracted him during their early rounds together. He told Tiger not to hit the ball in the water as Tiger was readying himself to swing. He coughed in the middle of Tiger's swing or tossed a ball in front of the one Tiger was aiming at. He dropped a bag of clubs down on the ground when Tiger was entering the impact zone. He imitated a crow's caw when Tiger was stroking a putt. Earl also had Tiger compete against older players to try to intimidate him, and start over if he missed one of four practice putts from around the hole. This type of boot-camp training by the former Green Beret lieutenant colonel made Tiger concentrate so intently that by age four nothing bothered him. It was at this time, in 1980, when Tiger was four, that Earl chose someone else to take over the reins and help Tiger play golf at even a higher level.

RUDY DURAN TAKES CHARGE OF TIGER

Rudy Duran, the head golf professional at the Heartwell Golf Course, in Southern California, had a reputation of being a fine teacher, particularly with junior players. Therefore, he seemed the perfect candidate to teach Tiger more advanced aspects of the swing and accelerate the learning process that was already moving at record pace.

Duran believed Tiger looked like a top PGA Tour pro in miniature swinging the club, so he simply reinforced the basics taught to Tiger earlier by his father and only made minor changes to Tiger's technique. These tweaks included shortening Tiger's backswing and changing his grip from a full-finger to an interlock hold. Duran also improved Tiger's balance by having him practice a unique drill.

"I used to have Tiger hit a shot then hold the finish position until the ball stopped rolling. Not only did this drill train Tiger to feel and repeat an on-balance swing, it disciplined him to be mentally tough," says Duran.

Although Duran played a somewhat minor role in changing Tiger's swing, he played a vital role in helping

Tiger strengthen his mental game. Duran encouraged Tiger to play Heartwell, knowing that Tiger would shoot low scores on this short, par-three golf course and build confidence. On the longer courses, Duran gave each hole a *Tiger-Par,* for example, changing a long par-four hole into a par six, to further help Tiger play more confidently.

During their rounds together, Duran advised Tiger to concentrate on playing one shot at a time and not worry about any previous bad shots or a difficult shot he would inevitably have to play later in the round. He also taught him to use his brain when selecting a club—for example, to play a stronger golf club when hitting an approach shot (or tee shot on a par three) to an elevated green, and one less club when playing to a green below sea level.

Tiger's focus was already very intense because of what he had learned from his father about honing in on the target mentally and concentrating on the basic elements of the setup and swing. However, under Duran, Tiger grew even stronger mentally, and this skill allowed him to become a better swinger and scorer. In fact, by age ten, when Duran left Tiger and moved on to the Chalk Mountain Golf Club in Atascadero, California, Tiger had already won two Junior World ten-and-under championships.

ENTER JOHN ANSELMO,
TIGER'S NEW TEACHER

In 1986, Earl Woods passed the torch to John Anselmo, the head teaching pro at Los Alamitos Golf Course in Cypress, California, near Tiger's home. Anselmo taught Tiger there for about a year. He then changed bases, moving to Meadowlark Golf Course in Huntington Beach, California, where he continued instructing the talented youngster.

Like Duran, Anselmo had a superb reputation as an instructor, particularly of junior golfers. Tiger's father made it clear that he wanted Anselmo to take Tiger's swing and shot-making game to the next level. Reflecting on being asked to help Tiger improve, Anselmo admits to feeling a little like a house painter being asked to redo the ceiling frescoes of the Sistine Chapel or a casual hiker being asked to lead a Mount Everest expedition. "Not because I lacked confidence in my teaching, but because I wondered what in the world I could possibly do for this golfing Mozart," says Anselmo.

It was not long before Anselmo began relying on instructional phrases that were very much like Yogi Berraisms, because they made Tiger think deeply. "Don't try hard; try to be fluid," "The ball is not to be hit, but directed," and "Hit with your practice swing" were three of Anselmo's favorite one-liners.

Anselmo was a big believer in playing lessons, too. So he and Tiger would play together at Meadowlark or the nearby Navy Golf Course, at which time Tiger would be taught the importance of staying on an even keel no matter how he played. Anselmo told Tiger that it was best not to overreact to a bad shot or get superexcited about a good shot—the reason being that drastic emotional swings negatively affect your concentration and thus hinder the way you will play your upcoming shot. If you overreact to a bad shot and hold on to that mental baggage, chances are you will make a faulty swing and hit a bad shot next. If you overreact to a good shot, the tendency is to become lackadaisical on the next shot and hit the ball off-line.

Anselmo also depended on mental imagery to enhance Tiger's swing and shot-making game. For example, to get Tiger to stand correctly to the ball, slightly bent over at the knees and ball-and-socket joints of the hips, Anselmo had Tiger visualize a posture somewhere between a soldier's address and at-ease positions.

To get Tiger out of the habit of swinging on a flat plane, as if he were in a giant teacup, and to swing on a more upright arc, he told Tiger to imagine swinging in a giant water glass.

To get Tiger to swing powerfully through impact in an uninhibited fashion, he instructed Tiger to look through the ball, from back to front, and down the target line rather than down at the ball.

To get Tiger to employ a rhythmic pitching-swing, marked by extra-smooth arm action, he had Tiger imagine a mother rocking a baby back and forth and swinging a range ball basket in the same manner.

To help Tiger take his mind off a water hazard fronting the green when playing short iron shots, he instructed him to imagine a colorful flag blowing at the very top of the flagstick and aim for it.

To make sure Tiger got the ball to the hole on slow greens or on uphill putts, he told him to pretend he was hitting to a second hole a few feet behind the real one.

Anselmo also helped Tiger improve his setup and swing by showing him old photographs of Sam Snead. Anselmo believes Snead to be the all-time best swinger technically. So he had Tiger visualize Snead's greatest moves before physically trying to copy specific setup, backswing, and downswing positions. This kind of unique training helped Tiger evolve more quickly into a superswinger and thus become more confident.

Although Anselmo was pro-Snead, he also encouraged Tiger to study former great players who used their imaginations to enhance their games—legends such as Bobby Jones, Ben Hogan, Jack Nicklaus, and Seve Ballesteros. Studying the thinking processes of legendary pros was part of the learning process. Moreover, this education reinforced what Tiger had learned about the relationship between the mind and golf and also taught him new ways to use his head on the course. These same words of wisdom, when applied to your own game will help you improve at an accelerated rate.

Bobby Jones

Jones grew up in a golfing family; however, he learned the importance of using the mind on the course from Stewart Maiden, a golf professional whom he frequently watched play and conversed with at Atlanta's East Lake Country Club. Jones, in his book *Bobby Jones on Golf,* says, "We want to know why a player, say John Smith, fails to play as well as John Smith ought to play with whatever skill he possesses. Obviously having eliminated every other variable, there is only John Smith's mind to look into, and this is where John Smith should look more often."

According to Anselmo, the most impressive points made by Jones about the mental side of golf, which all had a positive influence on Tiger, included:

1. Concentrate on only one swing thought, while keeping another in reserve, to help you feel more mentally secure.
2. Recall a good shot played previously from a similar lie or similar pressure situation to make you more relaxed and confident.
3. Stay on an even keel mentally throughout the round, no matter whether you score birdie, par, or bogey on a particular hole.

Ben Hogan

Ben Hogan developed a serious golfing mind-set in a very unique way. After a car crash in 1949 caused him to be bedridden, he retreated into a shell and figured out a way to hit a supercontrolled power fade shot instead of a hook that plagued him. One of his secrets was imagining a pane of glass, inclining upward from the ball through the shoulders, and keeping the arms and club below the glass in all stages of the backswing. This mental image allowed him to swing on not quite so flat a plane and made it easier for him to hit a left-to-right controlled shot. Hogan also depended on the feel in his hands to help him arrive at impact with the clubface slightly open at impact, an important technical link to hitting the fade; however, the way he enhanced his feel proves this eccentric character was always thinking.

Hogan discovered that the great pianists drink ginger ale before a performance. Because of its effects on the kidneys, the ginger in the ale apparently prevents the hands from feeling fat and puffy. Hogan claimed that because this favorite drink of his allowed him to have more feel in his fingers, he was able to work the clubface into a slightly open impact position more easily and to hit controlled fade shots consistently.

From the time of his crash onward, Hogan became such a deep thinker on the course and concentrated so hard that he was oblivious to what scores his fellow players were shooting. Hogan played in such a shell of concentration that once, during the Masters, he did not even notice his playing partner score a hole in one. Hogan's strong powers of concentration allowed him to plan out shots, then convincingly execute that plan by splitting the fairway off the tee, hitting the ball dead in line with the target on approach shots, pitching and chipping the ball close to the hole, and sinking putts.

Hogan, nicknamed the Iceman and the Hawk due to his quiet on-course demeanor and intense stare, never took his eyes off the fairway on tee shots and the flagstick on approach shots.

Golf experts have accused Tiger of being cold and Hoganlike when competing in a major championship. This near-perfect match has something to do with the fact that Tiger's present coach Butch Harmon played with Hogan as a boy and has since passed on what he learned to Tiger. I'll go into the Hogan influence more in chapter 3.

Most pros believe it's best to concentrate intensely on the course; however, others, including tour pro Fred Couples, believe a more laid-back attitude is better. Couples, whom I worked with on the book *Total Shotmaking,* told me that staying mentally carefree was one of his secrets to good play: "I'm not saying you should whistle *Summertime* while you're hitting shots. But I do think that when you're carefree, you're relaxed, and when you're relaxed you swing freely. All of which means you are going to generate maximum club-head speed on drives. On irons, you'll be less apt to steer the shot, which is one of the most common faults among club-level players."

Jack Nicklaus

Growing up and playing golf at a Donald Ross–designed course, Scioto Country Club in Columbus, Ohio, had a lot to do with Nicklaus's evolving into a logical and intelligent mental strategist who still claims he never misses a shot in his mind before swinging the club. In Nicklaus's heyday of the 1960s, he had such a mental edge that his fellow players believed they were playing for second place.

Scioto, like all Ross courses, is known for relatively narrow fairways bordered by lush rough, undulating crowned greens, plus penal bunkers and manicured expanses of grass called "collection areas" surrounding the putting surfaces. So it was especially important for Nicklaus to drive the ball in the fairway. But it was even more vital, on approach shots, that he pick the right club and swing at the precise speed to propel the ball to an area of the green that was level or else the ball was likely to roll off the sloping surface. Because of this strict shot-making criterion, Nicklaus was forced to get the yardage exactly right, focus hard on the target, concentrate on making sure his body and the club were aligned correctly, and take the time to patiently visualize a perfectly played shot.

Nicklaus's ability to use his head on the course and give each shot full concentration helped him win eighteen major championships, his last the Masters in 1986, plus a total of seventy PGA Tour events and ten Senior PGA Tour tournaments.

Even today, when Nicklaus prepares to hit a shot, the wheels in his brain turn so much that he says he "mentally goes to the movies." Before swinging, he actually is witness to an in-color cinematic flick playing in his head that includes frames showing the flight path of the shot and its trajectory, the ball landing on the green, and Nicklaus making the swing that will produce what was in his mental storyboards.

"I never hit a shot, even in practice, without having a very sharp, in-focus picture of it in my head," said Nicklaus in *Golf My Way,* his best-selling instruction book.

"Frankly, those amateurs I play with in pro-ams seem to have the club at the ball and their feet planted before they start 'seeing' pictures of the shot in their mind's eye."

Tiger idolizes Nicklaus for his great play over the years, for the major championship and scoring records he holds and that Tiger wants to break, and for his unique approach to the game. Even during press conferences, when reviewing a round, Tiger sounds like Jack when he says, "I just see the shot and hit it."

Severiano Ballesteros
Severiano Ballesteros, the swashbuckling Spanish golfer, took command of a championship course with the confi-

dence of a matador taking command of the bull in the ring. When working on the book *Natural Golf* with Ballesteros, I had the opportunity to play with him and witness for myself the value of intense mental focus. I could see just by the way he focused his eyes on the ball first, then the target second, that his imagination was running wild. Watching him, I just knew that he was going to hit a solid, creative shot and the ball was going to land close to the hole.

In conversations with this great champion, I also gained insight into the inner workings of his golfing brain. Ballesteros explained to me that he played in a bubble of intense concentration, a place where he tempered his will, gathered his thoughts, and planned strategies and shots with no outside interference. During our talks, Ballesteros admitted entering the bubble as early as three weeks prior to the start of a major. Like clockwork, a cloud came over him and grew even denser as the championship dates grew closer. When in this state of mind, he became so busy shoring himself up mentally to play winning golf that he told me people seemed to be talking to him through a pane of glass. By the time the tournament commenced, he was so deeply immersed in his game plan and play that he was virtually oblivious to outside sights and sounds. He was in such a solitary world that he often did not hear the gallery applauding or the clubs of his playing partners rattling when the caddy moved the bag holding them.

Thanks to Ballesteros's unique early training, he evolved

into a shot-making virtuoso, and this skill, developed while concentrating in a bubble, allowed him to win five major championships: three British Open and two Masters titles.

According to Seve, as he is still known to golfers around the world, since he was a boy learning the game with one club, a three iron, he felt most comfortable in this bubble. In fact, one-club practice is what taught him to concentrate so intently that he entered the bubble. One-club practice is also what taught him to use his imagination while in the bubble state and learn to hit a variety of shots by doing such things as opening or closing the clubface, gripping the club more firmly or lightly, and choking up or down on the club.

As good a short-game player as Ballesteros is, he told me he could be better had he learned with a seven-iron instead of a three iron. Ballesteros explained to me that the seven iron is the ideal club for ingraining good technique and a fine sense of touch. The club's comparatively short shaft and upright lie angle promote a controlled swinging action on the proper plane. Furthermore, and most important, the seven iron's thirty-nine degrees of loft induce confidence about easily getting the ball well up into the air.

Ironically, the seven iron was Tiger's first club, too. This is one chief reason why Tiger is so superconfident and imaginative when playing short pitch-and-chip shots from around the green.

When it comes to playing with superconcentration,

Tiger's all-business attitude is reminiscent of Ballesteros's during his heyday, with one exception: Tiger plays with even more intensity than Ballesteros played with when entering the bubble. Developing this skill obviously had something to do with Anselmo, when you consider that during the time he taught Tiger, Tiger won numerous championships. His most notable victories: the 1988, '89, '90, and '91 World Junior Championships, and the '91, '92, and '93 U.S. Junior Amateur.

If Jones, Hogan, Nicklaus, and Ballesteros each earned a master's degree in mental on-course aptitude, one professional and one professional alone—Tiger Woods—earned a Ph.D. This honored degree has a whole lot to do with Earl Woods, Rudy Duran, and John Anselmo, but more to do with Tiger's mother, Tida, a Buddhist, and clinical psychologist Dr. Jay Brunza. Tida worked quietly behind the scenes with her son, while Brunza kept tabs on what Anselmo was teaching, so that he could help Tiger use his mental skills to understand a specific swing movement and concentrate on grooving it.

In the upcoming chapter, you will learn how Brunza's Western teachings on the psychology of golf melded well with the Eastern teachings of Tiger's mother, who worked doggedly to help Tiger intensify his concentration skills and become enlightened. Each one of these low-profile individuals deserves credit for helping Tiger learn to enter the zone, a magical place where he concentrates one-pointedly.

THINK LIKE TIGER

- Respect the mental side of the game as Tiger does.
- Encourage your golfing children to watch good golfers' swings, the way Tiger watched his father's, and professionals' too, so they form an image of a technically sound technique in their mind.
- Learn to concentrate hard on the course so that nothing short of thunder and lightning disturbs you.
- Use your head, not your heart or pride, when choosing a club.
- Devise your own personal par score to ultimately increase your confidence.
- Be a student of the game, like Tiger, and learn from golf's legends.
- Like Bobby Jones and Tiger, concentrate on one swing key but keep a second in reserve.
- Like Ben Hogan and Tiger, give each shot 100 percent concentration.
- Like Jack Nicklaus and Tiger, "go to the movies" before you swing and see a perfectly played shot play in your mind's eye.
- As Seve Ballesteros and Tiger did, improvise with one club in practice to raise the level of your concentration and learn new shots.

2.

MIND, BODY, AND SPIRIT

In unraveling the mystery behind Tiger's
superior mental talent, I discovered some
"deep" shortcuts to playing good golf.

BEFORE CONDUCTING RESEARCH FOR THIS BOOK, I wondered how Tiger had become so good at golf— so much better than anyone who had ever played the game, including Jack Nicklaus. Oh, I knew Tiger was blessed with talent, through good genes. I also knew that his father's being a good golfer and personal coach helped him greatly, as did swing and shot-making tips he received from supremely talented instructors. You now know as much as I do about all that previous history. What you don't know about are those things that have been kept secret, involving Tiger's connections to the mind, body, and spirit.

Let me now lead you through the door of intrigue. Join me in unraveling the true mystery of how Tiger heightened his mental awareness, toned his body into tip-top shape, and took his game to such a sophisticated level that his superior play seems spiritual in nature, and losing never enters his mental equation.

THE MIND

Golf is 90 percent mental. The other 10 percent is mental.

JIM FLICK One of *Golf* magazine's
Top 100 Teachers in America

Had Tiger just learned golf from superteachers Rudy Duran, John Anselmo, and Butch Harmon, that would have been enough of an advantage; however, that was not the case. Thanks to a father who wanted to do everything in his power to help his son realize his lifelong dream of becoming golf's best player ever, Tiger was given a broad-scoped education. Tiger's learning experience went far beyond being taught the fundamental positions of the setup and swing and the basics of course management and mental toughness. Remember: Earl is a former Green Beret with a never-say-die attitude, so he was not going to let anything stand in his way. His goal: to train Tiger as no other golfer before him had been trained, including the great Jack Nicklaus.

A good golfer in his own right, Earl knew the importance of Tiger's being given high-level instruction from experienced teachers. Being an action man, however, Earl took things into his own hands when it came to helping Tiger evolve into a human golfing machine. Showing more determination than an obsessed Russian Olympic gymnastics coach, he brought friend Captain Jay Brunza, a Navy clinical psychologist, into Tiger's inner circle. This is when Tiger's approach to the mental game of golf really started to change dramatically.

I first heard about the "doctor" when reading an article on Tiger that appeared in *USA Weekend,* July 24–26, 1992, in which Brunza was quoted as saying: "Tiger is so advanced mentally, it's scary. I did some sports psychology with athletes at the (U.S.) Naval Academy where we worked on things like ways to focus attention, and Tiger is far ahead of anything I've ever seen."

Something about this statement, which I perceived as downright vague, struck a chord in my brain and made me think there was something cryptic being said in between the lines. I was suddenly curious, very curious indeed. Questions flashed through my brain. What methods did Brunza use to induce midshipmen to focus? Did Brunza use the same techniques on Tiger? Could Brunza's psychological method involve the "it" word—*hypnosis?* Were

Tiger's advanced mental skills, developed through Brunza, responsible for his domination on the junior golf circuit?

At the time the article in *USA Weekend* was published, I was working at *Golf* magazine, and my job as senior editor of instruction was to conjure up ideas for articles that would help golfer-readers improve their game. I could smell a big story, so at our next editorial meeting I suggested to George Peper, the magazine's editor-in-chief, that I look into exactly what Brunza was up to. Peper pooh-poohed the idea, however, even though Tiger had just become both the medalist (low scorer in the qualifying round) and match-play winner of the 1992 U.S. Junior Amateur. He believed there was too little to go on. Besides, he felt strongly that sports psychologists all say the same things and use a lot more words than they have to. Consequently, as far as investigating my hunch further was concerned, I was stopped in my tracks. Still, I thought that in my spare time I would pursue what I considered a lead. I got sidetracked, however, writing other articles and golf instructional books.

Years passed, and, to be honest, I forgot about Brunza until 1997 when I read *Tiger Woods—The Makings of a Champion*. In this excellently written book, the author, Tim Rosaforte, comes right out and says what I had sensed five years earlier: Dr. Jay Brunza had hypnotized Tiger.

"Hypnotism was next," wrote Rosaforte. "Brunza could put Woods into a trance in less than a minute."

At the time Rosaforte's book hit the stands, Tiger had just won the 1997 Masters, one of the most coveted major championships, by a record-shattering twelve shots. Normal pro golfers just don't win big tournaments by that kind of margin. Questions began popping into my head. Could Tiger's mental mastery, resulting from his work with Brunza, be the paramount reason he had dominated amateur golf and was now dominating professional golf? Even though I knew Rosaforte as an excellent writer with an eye for news, were the statements and colorful anecdotes about hypnosis mentioned in his book true? And, if so, was it fair for Tiger to coast mentally while other tour pros were forced to deal with demons and play through fear and anxiety? Perplexed, I wanted to get to the truth; however, I realized that getting to the bottom of this story would not be easy, especially since Earl Woods never made any mention of hypnosis in his book *Training a Tiger* that also came out in 1997. Moreover, although Rudy Duran, John Anselmo, and Butch Harmon are talked about in this book, there is not one mention of Brunza. Furthermore, because Brunza was considered a member of what Tida Woods called "Team Tiger," I wondered if the intention was to keep Tiger's hypnotism a secret, knowing that this training might be perceived as the missing link to Tiger's exceptional play. I decided to dismiss the idea of a cover-up, concluding that the reason for secrecy had to do simply with the confidentiality factor that encompasses all doctor-patient relationships. Eventually, all my questions—including how hypnosis can help one's golf game—would be answered; however, that would not be until early in the new millennium when I conceived the idea to write this book.

In conducting my investigative work, I decided to go right to the horse's mouth, as they say. Knowing that John Anselmo and Brunza had worked hand and hand during Tiger's winning days as a junior, I asked Anselmo for Brunza's telephone number.

In my first conversation with Brunza, in late July 2000, I started off by saying that during the 2000 British Open Tiger didn't seem phased by anything—even on the last day of the championship when on his way to victory the huge gallery following him was going wild. Tiger seemed to be floating, I said. He was in such a rhythm that nothing could stop him.

While sitting at my desk waiting for Brunza to comment, I flashed back to 1976, when I set a course record sixty-eight at Long Island's Crab Meadow Golf Course. On that magical day, I played in a trance, so I knew that the "zone" was something real. Next, I flashed back to the 2000 British Open thinking that I had never seen any player look like Tiger, so out of it but so in the game. If you ever watch the video of that championship, particularly the footage of the last day, as I went back and did, you will not believe what you see. More than ever, I now wanted to know if Brunza had trained Tiger, through hypnosis, how to click into a superclear, superpositive, heightened sense of relaxed concentration.

Once having broken the silence, Brunza talked about all the help he had given Tiger and seemed to be upset about being let go suddenly. Brunza had been Tiger's on-course psychological guide and caddy during many junior and amateur events that he won, including the 1991, 1992, and 1993 U.S. Junior Amateur and the 1994 and 1995 U.S. Amateur. In total, Brunza caddied for Tiger during thirty-nine matches. Together, they won thirty-three. Regardless of their successful partnership, Brunza told me that during the 1996 U.S. Amateur, Tiger switched to caddy Byron Bell, a best friend from Western High. Tiger felt Brunza was more useful as a mental coach, helping him focus. Ironically, Tiger won the U.S. Amateur that year, but Brunza was let go. Upon hearing this, I could have easily jumped to the conclusion that hypnosis must have played a major role in Tiger's success, and someone in his camp wanted to keep this a secret. But instead I chose to ask Brunza straight out if he had ever hypnotized Tiger. He said he would get back to me.

During the several-month hiatus, between the time I telephoned Brunza and the time he telephoned me, I decided to find out more about hypnosis. Let me share with you the consensus of what I learned (from reading books, consulting with experts, and talking to golf pros familiar with the benefits of hypnosis) just in case you, like so many laymen, believe hypnosis to be a voodoolike vehicle for turning people into chickens and pigs and having them make jerks of themselves on stage.

The actual process of hypnosis involves putting a person into a trancelike state and then suggesting how he or she can make positive changes. In Tiger's case, these changes obviously involved the game of golf, and he, like all "patients," had to be willing to accept suggestions for improvement. Dr. Jay Brunza or any other trained hypnotist cannot hypnotize someone against his or her will.

When being hypnotized, an individual is asked to close his eyes and focus on his body while breathing slowly. Next, the hypnotist usually depends on an induction, like saying "Your hands are getting heavier," to lead the person into a trance. Having said that, when a person becomes hypnotized he is not out of it. He enters a heightened state of awareness that allows him to let go totally, both physically and mentally. This explains why hypnotized people feel that their bodies are "heavy" and their minds superalert and willing to be open to positive suggestions. Hypnotized people are aware of everything that is going on around them, but are so tuned in to the hypnotist's voice that they sink into the subconscious and erase negative thoughts and emotions that had previously hindered their concentration and, if they are golfers, their performance on the course.

The hypnotist often leads a person out of his trance by having him imagine he is walking slowly down a flight of stairs or out of a tunnel. He keeps "walking" until he is ready to step down or walk out into the light at the end of the tunnel.

Hypnosis is a science, and one you can teach yourself, as I learned from Dr. Jay Brunza when he telephoned me back. Regarding this second conversation with Brunza, I recall him admitting to working with Tiger, confirming Rosaforte's statements. I could tell from the tone of Brunza's voice that he felt much more comfortable, and proud, talking about how he had helped Tiger help himself.

"Tiger is now understanding and applying *all* the high-level mental game keys that I provided him with for so many years," said Brunza. "He's now mature enough, too, to comprehend the finer points of putting himself into a zone of intense concentration during a round of golf."

As soon as I heard these words of Brunza's, I understood the depth of two comments made by Tiger Woods during two separate interviews on *Larry King Live:*

"I don't talk that much to my fellow players because I'm too busy concentrating, in my own world taking care of business," said Tiger on June 10, 1998.

"I stay in the present, focusing on what I need to accomplish in the here and now," said Tiger on February 27, 2000.

You can click yourself back into a hypnotic state, and put into action the positive suggestions made previously by a hypnotist, just by repeating a code word, phrase, number, physical gesture, or recalling an image that was given to you by the hypnotist. Brunza did not reveal any code to me. Still, Mike Austin, renowned teaching pro and *Guinness Book of World Records* holder for the longest drive ever (515 yards), believes Tiger uses one. Austin, who studied abnormal psychology at the University of Georgia, knows how to administer hypnosis, plus he's been hypnotized himself. "Tiger Woods plays in a trance," said Austin. "As someone who has studied hypnotism and hypnotized golfers myself, I can tell by looking at Tiger that he uses a posthypnotic code to put himself in the zone."

"I don't know about a code, but I do know about an *indicator,*" says golf pro Ray Oakes. Oakes told me that he let himself be hypnotized by Brunza after hearing from his friend Earl Woods how Tiger's mental focus and shot-making imagination improved rapidly after just the first of many sessions with Brunza, starting at age ten. When out on the course, following his hypnotic session with Brunza, Oakes said he recalled the white carpet image or indicator Brunza had given him. Instantly, all the positive suggestions, such as "You have a job to do, hit the ball accurately," came back to him. "I slipped into such a state of relaxed confidence that I actually could see a vivid image of a white carpet running down the fairway. No fear of hitting the ball off line entered my mind and, as a result, I played great golf."

My guess, after studying Tiger, is that closing his eyes very slowly, then opening them just as slowly, two or three times, is Tiger's indicator. I say this because I have seen him do this so many times in the course of a competitive round of golf.

Whether I am right about Tiger's code is not important. What's important is that you understand the inner workings of the doctor-patient relationship. It's also important for you to realize that you can put yourself into a hypnotic state, even though you have never visited a hypnotist. To sink into a trance, simply do the following:

1. Breathe slowly.
2. Let your body relax more with each breath, until it goes limp.
3. Accept suggestions that you give to yourself, such as: "When I step onto the first tee to drive, I will think of nothing else but relaxing my muscles and hitting the ball down the middle of the fairway."

Thanks to Dr. Jay Brunza, Tiger's mind is in the right place most of the time on the course, and that asset allows him to give each shot-making situation full concentration. "Tiger has no equal when it comes to focus," says Dr. Fran Pirozzolo, who is the mind manager of the New York Yankees baseball team and former mentor to heavyweight boxing champion Evander Holyfield. "Tiger plays within a shell of concentration that cracks open only after he wins the championship he's playing in, usually with a record score." Once I knew how Brunza had helped Tiger, I also found it easier to comprehend how Tiger could maintain his concentration while bouncing a ball off the face of the club, over and over on a Nike commercial that you have surely seen. If not, he's so mentally cool that he works the golf club and bouncing ball behind his back and between his legs. No wonder Nike pays this guy millions. He's as su-perfocused as a tiger going after prey, on and off the golf course, and that is a credit to Brunza and others who have helped him develop his powers of concentration.

I believe hypnosis is at least part of the reason for Tiger's supreme mental fortitude that encompasses his will to win and his love of coming from behind to snatch victory as he did in the 2001 World Golf Championship NEC Invitational. Tiger was two strokes behind fellow PGA Tour player Jim Furyk going into the final round. Not only did Tiger catch him and force a playoff, but he also won that playoff after looking like he was dead a couple of times. Tiger simply dug down deep, shut out all negative thoughts, stayed superpositive, and pulled out the win, as he also did in both the 2002 Masters and U.S. Open cham-pionships.

When all the fat is boiled off, though, I do not believe, as I once did, that hypnosis is an elixir. If you are a weekend hacker, you just can't visit the hypnotist once and expect to be turned into a scratch golfer. One hundred visits won't do the trick either. I'm glad that's true, because if it were not,

I'd have to side with old-school pros such as my friend Ken Venturi who believes it is essentially a way of cheating.

I do believe that hypnosis can help you greatly to eliminate demons that cause you to distrust yourself, get very nervous on the first tee, or employ a nervous "yip-stroke." Sessions with a hypnotherapist can also lift you up mentally and help you hit top-quality shots consistently—provided that you possess a fundamentally sound swing technique and putting stroke.

One major reason why hypnotism has gotten such a bad rap is that golfers are uninformed. Other than Mike Austin, Ray Oakes, and Laird Small, one of the top 100 best teachers in America according to *Golf* magazine, golfers have kept their "therapy" to themselves. I guess golfers who have been hypnotized feel that the public will get the wrong idea. This, I'm told, is the reason why Muhammad Ali kept quiet about going to a hypnotist while he was beating up boxers year after year.

The question you might still ask yourself is "Why hasn't Tiger gone back to Brunza?" I guess it's because the problems he has from time to time with his game are no longer mental, as Rich Lerner of The Golf Channel confirmed. "No golfer matches the mental game of Tiger Woods," says Learner. But, even if Lerner's words are an exaggeration, and Tiger does experience a mental block occasionally, he can revert back to the lessons his mother gave him and what he continues to learn at the Buddhist temple about the value of meditation. You, too, will learn these same lessons, but first let's look at the value of taking care of the body. Physical fitness is very important to Tiger and should be a priority of yours, because a good body makes for a good mind and spirit.

THE BODY

The golfer's body demands quality nutrients to carry out the proper physical and mental control.

NINA ANDERSON, CHERIE TRIPP, AND
DR. HOWARD PEIPER, authors of
Nutritional Leverage for Great Golf

When a superfit Tiger Woods won the 1997 Masters, at age twenty-one, and started dominating golf at the start of the new millennium, tour professionals around the world realized that the bar had been raised and to compete they, too, had to become more health conscious. Colin Montgomerie from Scotland, Sergio Garcia from Spain, Darren Clarke from Ireland, Thomas Bjorn from Denmark, Shigeki Maruyama from Japan, and David Duval from the United States were part of a long list of professional golfers who joined the get-in-shape bandwagon. All these professionals have since learned that a healthful diet and exercise program are vital links to feeling better about oneself and becoming more confident, swinging the club more fluidly, hitting more solid shots, and thinking more clearly on the course—things Tiger learned long ago.

Tiger's parents have always been health conscious. Besides, Tiger had been made fully aware of other fitness-minded past golf champions, namely South African Gary Player, Australian Greg Norman, Spaniard Seve Ballesteros, and Englishman Nick Faldo. Teacher John Anselmo made sure of that.

THE GARY PLAYER INFLUENCE

In terms of dedication, Tiger is the one modern-day player who matches Gary Player.

Player, a South African professional small in stature, competed at the highest level with the likes of Arnold Palmer and Jack Nicklaus. Palmer was naturally athletic, built sort of like Sean Connery, who played James Bond in the Ian Fleming movies. Nicklaus was simply big and strong, Player's ability to beat these two golfing powerhouses and win championships had little to do with natural talent and a lot to do with willpower, diligent practice, and most of all a disciplined diet and fitness program.

During his heyday, Player was only five feet seven inches tall and weighed 155 pounds, yet he was all muscle and a positive thinker. He knew then what he knows now: A healthy body and mind developed through regular exercise get the heart pumping and clear out the cobwebs from the brain. To stay healthy, Player stuck to a diet of fish, chicken, pasta, vegetables, and whole-wheat bread and snacked on dried fruits, bananas, nuts, and raisins.

He enhanced his mind by crossing his legs in the classic yoga position and breathing slowly and deeply until he put himself into a relaxed meditative state.

As Player discovered, and you will too, yoga is a form of meditation that unites the body, mind, and spirit. So regular practice will help you think more clearly on the course and thus reduce mental errors that are all-too-familiar score wreckers.

A favorite yoga exercise of mine and among practitioners such as Player is the *Butterfly Pose*. This exercise is used to stretch the body and increase mental energy and can be employed by taking the following steps:

STEP 1: Sit down, ideally on a mat, then bring the soles of your feet together.

STEP 2: Clasp your feet with your hands and bring them as close to your body as is comfortably possible.

STEP 3: Open your chest by pushing your shoulder blades together.

STEP 4: Drop your head toward your feet, ideally enough to rest it on your hands. (If this feels uncomfortable, remain in the position you were in after completing the previous step.)

STEP 5: Hold the position for a full thirty seconds as you inhale and exhale. Again, to get the full benefit of this exercise, let your belly expand as you inhale and bring your navel toward your spine as you exhale. In this psychic shell, picture the ideal golf swing, then carry this image with you to the golf course.

PLAYER ENHANCED HIS BODY AND INDIRECTLY HIS mind by skipping rope and working out with weights. His favorite physical exercise was gripping the metal bar of a ten-pound dumbbell like a golf club, then making a swing motion. This exercise strengthens the muscles of the hands, arms, and shoulders that are all so vital to good golf. Player was such a fanatic that he also squeezed a tennis ball when traveling by jet to golf tournaments and did fingertip pushups in his hotel room once he arrived in the area where a competition was being held. Whatever exercise Player did, he concentrated hard on moving slowly and methodically, knowing from experience that this disciplined routine encouraged him to take the same care when setting up to the ball and preparing to swing.

To shorten a long story, Player went on to become one of the all-time great golfers, recognized most for being one of only five men to win all four major championships. The others who have attained this feat are Gene Sarazen, Ben Hogan, Jack Nicklaus, and Tiger Woods.

Regardless of Player's success, golfers who competed against him in the '50s, '60s, and '70s never took exercise seriously, and practicing yoga was farthest from their minds. Even later on, in the 1980s, when Greg Norman, Seve Ballesteros, and Nick Faldo proved the dynamic relationship between staying physically fit and being able to clearly focus on the golf course—and win major championships—the fitness bug failed to catch on among tour players. This made no difference to the aforesaid trio. They had discovered one of the secrets to playing well and were laughing all the way to the bank, winning seventeen major championships among them.

THE NORMAN INFLUENCE

Norman's success as a pro, taking lessons from Harmon, influenced Tiger's decision to go with same teacher in 1993. Harmon has always believed that a player must be fit to play good golf, and it is obvious from looking at Tiger's physique that Harmon has always had a positive influence on Tiger.

One of Norman's favorite exercises, even today, is "swinging" a medicine ball. He simply sets up as if he is going to hit a ball (arms hanging down naturally, weight balanced between both feet), but he holds the medicine ball rather than a club, then uses his torso to make a powerful turning motion and toss the ball. The main physical benefit of this exercise is that it helps you strengthen and tighten the abdomen. That can be a huge advantage, particularly to older players who have, for one reason or another, developed a beer belly that forces them to swing the club on an outside-inside path instead of an inside-inside one. If you've gained some weight in the midsection and think you can handle tossing a seven-pound medicine ball, give it a try; it might help you improve your swing.

The other benefit of the medicine ball exercise is developing a strong sense of mental focus. Norman told me that using his torso rather than his hands and arms to control the motion forced him to concentrate more intently on and off the golf course.

THE BALLESTEROS INFLUENCE

Only one player today plays with the same swashbuckling style of former great Severiano Ballesteros: Tiger Woods. And being a student of the game, Tiger surely knows that Ballesteros's fit body had a lot to do with his skills as a shot maker.

Ballesteros loved to ride a bicycle for miles through the Spanish countryside, because it gave him a good workout and allowed him to escape into a peaceful world of mental solitude.

THE FALDO INFLUENCE

Like Nick Faldo, Tiger is always striving for perfection in the swing. To match the most ideal swing positions consistently and hit the ball powerfully, you must be physically fit. Like Faldo, Tiger works hard to stay fit.

Faldo's exercise program was rigorous and involved Nautilus machine workouts. He always left a session feeling energized both physically and mentally, then took that supercharged body-mind attitude to the links.

Whichever workout program you choose is up to you and, ideally, a physical trainer. The important thing is that you build up a variety of muscles used in the golf swing, namely those in the hands, arms, hips, shoulders, and back, while concentrating very hard on what you're doing. The harder you focus off the course, the easier it will be to focus on the course.

TIGER WOODS:
THE GOLFING SUPERMAN

Today, Tiger is the ultimate athlete, who understands the relationship between diet, exercise, and mental clarity. Although he has been known to crave McDonald's hamburgers and french fries from time to time, you can tell that he eats healthful foods off the course just by looking at his strong and trim body. He even had a healthful Thai dish served at the Champions' Dinner at Augusta National Golf Club for Masters winners.

On the course, you'll see him drinking plenty of water, which makes sense, according to Nina Anderson, Cherie Tripp, and Dr. Howard Peiper, authors of *Nutritional Leverage for Great Golf,* who say: "Without water, the brain doesn't think and allow us to make judgments properly."

Tiger has been known to snack on a banana, too, because this fruit supplies us with potassium that is vital to the muscles and necessary for enhancing concentration.

Tiger has made an effort to keep his exact fitness routine secret, but it's known that his workouts include weight training, stretching, running, and other types of aerobic work.

Doing bench presses has helped Tiger bulk up his biceps and upper body quite a lot. In fact, he looks as fit as Sugar Ray Leonard did when he beefed up, entered the light-middleweight division, and beat Marvin Hagler for the title. No wonder Tiger hits drives and iron shots a country mile and rips the ball out of the deepest rough.

Tiger also hits the ball powerfully due to a strong turn developed through stretching. According to Mark Russell of the PGA Tour, when not signing autographs, talking to the media, or practicing, Tiger visits the Cintenela Fitness Trailer, a fixture at tournaments sites, to work on stretching exercises, either by himself or with a certified physical trainer. Doing stretching exercises helps him stay superflexible, and, in turn, this physical asset allows him to make a strong body turn when he swings and to generate great clubhead speed and distance. Russell also told me that, when in the on-site fitness trailer, Tiger also keeps his legs strong by working on the treadmill and stationary bike.

When off the tour, I'm told Tiger runs. Running also helps Tiger keep his legs toned. The legs must be strong to stabilize the winding and unwinding actions of the body during the swing and protect you from feeling fatigued when walking a hilly course in competition. Running is also a fine heart-strengthening aerobic exercise. Running enhances your sense of balance and forces you to concentrate on timing and rhythm. Most important, running stimulates the brain and enables you to focus clearly on the course.

To understand another vital benefit of running (or jogging or walking), take a break from your busy at-home or work schedule and get those legs moving. You'll see immediately how the second you begin exercising and activate the endorphins in your brain, your thinking process will become sharper. The secret is to stay with this valuable exercise so that you feel more positive and carry this over to the golf course as Tiger does.

GOLF DRILL EXERCISES

Another form of exercise that has helped Tiger stay stronger in body and mind and become more agile and swing more efficiently is drill work on the practice tee. This kind of workout will help you improve your body, mind, and game, too, so let me review some practice drills taught to Tiger by John Anselmo and Butch Harmon before discussing the benefits of Buddhist meditation.

The *Range Bucket Drill* is an exercise that Anselmo taught Tiger to help him:

1. stretch his vital golf muscles in the back.
2. learn to swing in balance.
3. feel the pivot points of the swing.
4. feel the hinging action of the wrists vital to the swing.
5. bring out and exaggerate the natural to-and-fro motion that he believes we are all born with.
6. enhance his ability to concentrate by focusing on how various parts of the body work together to make a flowing, coordinated motion.

The next time you visit the driving range, take one of the empty range buckets in your hands and stand as you would to hit a ball. Grasp the left side of the bucket with the fingers of your left hand, the right side of the bucket with the fingers of your right.

Swing the basket back, concentrating on the arms swinging, muscles in your back stretching, and body weight shifting to your right foot and leg. More important, feel the wrists hinge naturally, the right more than the left. Make a mental note of this hinging action so you don't consciously try to hinge your wrists the next time you play. (Many amateurs who consciously cock the wrists on the backswing overdo things and cause the club to swing well beyond the parallel positon at the top. As a result, they unhinge the wrists too early in the downswing, lose power, and tend to misdirect the club through impact.)

Once your hips and shoulders are wound up and you've swung the basket above your head, rotate your left hip counterclockwise until you straighten your left leg and begin using it as a firm post to uncoil around. As you continue uncoiling your hips, make a mental note of how the arms swing down automatically. Now you know why Tiger's swing is so powerful. He lets his body operate on automatic pilot. He does not try to force the body to work, as so many high handicappers do.

Anselmo taught Tiger the *Looking Glass Drill* to help him check his technique. During the eight years that Tiger took lessons from Anselmo, the California-based teacher used to have him set up and swing in front of a pane-glass window in the nearby clubhouse at the Meadowlark Golf Course in Huntington Beach, California.

Once you learn the basics, check your address position in a mirror. Next, swing and stop at different stages, then stare at these images in the mirror for about ten seconds as Tiger was instructed to do. Forming a mental picture of each swing position will allow you to store the correct movement into your brain's database. Whenever you play, call on these images and see how easy it is to make a smooth action and hit the ball far and straight.

The Eyes Shut, Open Mind Drill is a unique practice exercise that Butch Harmon learned from his father, Claude Harmon, Sr., then passed on to Tiger. Before you attempt to hit the ball, visualize the movements of the body and club. Actually see the backswing, downswing, and follow-through in your mind's eye, and picture the ball flying off the clubface. Next, set up to a ball and turn that mental movie into reality, as you swing at a real ball with your eyes closed. You'll be surprised when you make solid contact. Bring this imagery to the golf course, and you'll be a much better player.

Harmon also recommended that Tiger practice the *Slow But Sure Drill* to improve his swing tempo. One of the main problems all golfers run into is swinging too fast. I'm all for generating high club-head speed, as long as you can remain balanced and put the center of the clubface or "sweet spot" squarely on the ball at impact.

When Tiger first came to Harmon for lessons, his tempo was too fast. Having him swing at 75 percent of full speed encouraged him to learn the job descriptions of the feet, arms, hands, hips, and shoulders. As with anything else, the slower you do something complex, the more likely you will be able to remember what's involved and repeat it. More important, you will discover precisely how fast you can repeat the task (swing) while remaining patient.

THE SPIRIT

All that we are is the result of what we have thought.

SIDDHARTHA GAUTAMA, BUDDHA

I had already learned from Earl Woods, through written correspondence, that Tida Woods, Tiger's mother, had taught Tiger patience and tenacity, but I was curious to know if her belief in Buddhism had been passed on to him. So I decided to try to reach Tida through John Anselmo, knowing that they were close and she was a private person owing to her son's superstar status.

Anselmo phoned Tida and told her about the book I was writing. Through him, she relayed important information that no one in the golf world, not even Anselmo, knew about. Here's what I discovered from Anselmo's interview with Tida, who is from Thailand where Zen meditation is practiced.

When Tiger was a young boy, his mother gave him a gold Buddha chain. She also took him to a Buddhist temple, where he prayed with Zen masters and learned to put himself into a super-relaxed state of mind through deep concentration and what is referred to simply as "letting go." I also discovered that, these days, Tiger reports back to the California-based Buddhist temple for meditative tune-ups.

Meditation is exercise for the mind. The difference between hypnosis and meditation is this: When you meditate, you focus on yourself, as opposed to hypnosis, when you focus on suggestions from the hypnotist.

When one meditates, he or she usually sits comfortably in a lotus or half-lotus position, on a soft pillow, futon, or a thick meditation mat called a *zabuton*. Usually, too, during meditation the hands are kept in the lap, one under the other, with the thumbs touching. Additionally, the tongue is kept behind the mouth and breaths are taken slowly through the nose.

Zen Buddhist practitioners usually count slowly, stay in tune with the rhythm of their own breath, focus on an image such as a candle flame, or repeat a mantra. Others contemplate solving a riddle. One of these hooks leads the practitioner into a relaxed state, a "zone," if you will, where the mind and body let go and meld with the spirit. If you meditate yourself and slip into this altered state, you will feel as if all you see around you are raindrops falling, falling, falling, very s l o w l y down a windowpane. Everything slows down, including your body, which is in a super-relaxed state.

Ideally, through meditation, you will find enlightenment or *satori,* in the same way that Siddhartha Gautama (Buddha) did in the sixth century B.C. while meditating under a Bodhi tree. He learned to meditate from other truth seekers as Tiger did from his mother and other Buddhists.

When you gain wisdom through calming the mind, as Tiger has, you learn how to alleviate pressure, not simply deal with it. You also learn not to expect anything—good or bad. Instead, you learn that it is best to go with the flow of the body and mind and accept the results. By disciplining yourself to let go, which, again, is an important part of Buddhist teachings, you swing freely, rather than letting yourself think too much about technique and, as a result, tense up and make a faulty action.

Through meditation, Tiger has also learned to transcend the ego—I. That freedom has enabled him to open the door to spiritual enlightenment and experience harmony among the mind, body, and spirit. When this occurs, the mind's thinking process becomes crystal clear and the body relaxes. This explains why Tiger is able to vividly visualize shots and employ such an efficient golf swing.

Meditation also helps you overcome doubt and focus on

the moment, which explains why Tiger seems very cocky and aloof on the golf course. In reality, he's just positive and in the zone focusing one-pointedly with no distractions. The detached look on his face at the 2000 British Open indicated he was simply experiencing the sense of oneness with the universe that comes from meditation. Tiger's winning ways at the "British," as well as at other majors, can be attributed to his mother's influence and what he learned at Buddhist temples regarding a form of meditation called *Shamatha*. This meditation is concerned with developing a special kind of concentration—the keen ability to maintain intense focus on an object (e.g., the golf ball or golf target) with the greatest of ease, so that the practitioner's mind, body, and spirit become supercharged, virtually effortlessly. Shamatha has been known to release such paranormal powers as the ability to levitate or read people's minds. Tiger has not reached this stage of development; however, he certainly has levitated himself above his competitors by learning how to focus one-pointedly and hit shots no other golf professional would even attempt, let alone succeed, in hitting.

Tiger plays the game with such ease that's it's obvious his subconscious mind allows him to execute impossible-looking shots due to a stress-free state of mind and a super-confident attitude he learned through meditation and by working with Brunza.

Although Tiger has experience meditating, my research shows that you can concentrate so hard on the course that you can put yourself into a hypnotic state. The same thing happens to trout fishermen who listen to a gurgling brook.

Hogan and Nicklaus, both of whom rarely talked to anyone other than their caddies during competition, snapped themselves into a super state of concentration, much like Tiger's. You should, too, even if that means meditating or hypnotizing yourself before you play.

THINK LIKE TIGER

• Hypnosis could be the route to take if you want to block out negative thoughts that are hindering your ability to concentrate positively.

• Follow a regular diet and exercise program. Consider a high-protein diet, combined with a weight-lifting and stretching routine similar to Tiger's.

• Consider meditation to help you alleviate mental stress, relax your muscles, and improve your golf game. It works for Tiger, so it might help you.

3.

BUTCH HARMON'S INFLUENCE

Guru golf instructor Claude "Butch" Harmon taught
Tiger how to take his game to a higher level, by con-
centrating his mental energy on new setup and swing
positions and learning intelligent on-course strategies.

TIGER'S SECOND-ROUND LOSS TO PAUL PAGE IN the 1993 U. S. Amateur championship, played at the Champions Golf Club in Houston, Texas, proved to be a watershed in his career. In fact, the defeat motivated his father to set up a meeting right away with teacher Claude "Butch" Harmon, from the nearby Lochinvar Golf Club. Harmon, the son of 1948 Masters champion Claude Harmon, Sr., had already made a name for himself as the private teacher of King Hussan II of Morocco and by helping tour pros Greg Norman and Davis Love improve their swings.

Upset with his swing because it was causing him to occasionally hit score-wrecking hook shots, Tiger was looking for new tips that would turn his game around and bring his head up. He and his father hoped Harmon could spot the faults in his swing and correct them, namely because Tiger had dreams of winning the U.S. Amateur and turning pro. If those dreams were to be realized, Tiger needed a new swing that he felt positive about and could repeat consistently under pressure.

The meeting with Harmon was a good one. Harmon videotaped Tiger's swing and made some comments that were sometimes harsh, including this one: "Tiger, you're too much up on your right toe during the downswing. I want more of your right foot to stay on the ground and the heel of that foot to lead the toe the way Hogan's did. You're standing up on that right toe as if you were a ballet dancer. Until you stop it, you are going to continue to spin out on the downswing at least a couple of times in a round, lose your balance, hit those awful off-the-world drives that cost you double bogeys and tournaments, and maintain a negative mental attitude."

According to Harmon, Tiger felt encouraged and was about as optimistic as a weekend hacker who buys a new driver to lift his spirits or takes a lesson from a local pro for the first time. Tiger returned the next day, at which time Harmon presented him with an overview of what changes had to be made to his existing technique to turn him into a more consistent swinger and shot maker with a positive mind-set.

For the next several months, this new team talked technique over the telephone with Harmon offering constructive criticism after reviewing videos Tiger had sent him of his swing. Then, prior to the 1994 U.S. Amateur, Tiger returned twice to Lochinvar for lessons. Tiger felt very comfortable with the changes he had made to his swing, especially after getting the nod from his longtime coach, John Anselmo, who had faded out of the picture after a serious illness that he was eventually to recover from.

The early physical changes Harmon made to Tiger's setup and swing are documented in the book *The Four Cornerstones of Winning Golf*, which I co-authored with Harmon. These elementary-level changes included:

1. a wider stance (to help Tiger keep his right foot down longer on the downswing and make a better move through the ball)
2. a smaller hip turn (to build resistance between Tiger's upper and lower body and, in turn, create powerful torque in the swing)
3. a longer takeaway and higher hand position at the top (to enable Tiger to create a wide and powerful swing arc)
4. a shorter-length backswing (to enhance Tiger's control of the club)

5. a lateral bump with the hips on the downswing (to enhance Tiger's timing)

These swing changes also allowed Tiger to play better and compete with a stronger sense of self-confidence—factors that led to his winning three U.S. Amateur Championships in a row—in 1994, '95, and '96. Shortly thereafter, Tiger made the decision to turn pro, which shocked nobody. What did shock the golf world was a comment Tiger made about his game "not reaching A-game standard." Fans, golf writers, and touring pros around the world wondered, "How the heck can Tiger possibly improve?"

Only Harmon understood what Tiger meant: that as good as he was at golf, he needed to get better if he was going to dominate the pro circuit and earn the title of world's greatest pro golfer by winning major championships. Tiger did just that, with the help of Harmon, who spent hours teaching Tiger at Rio Seco, his new home base in Las Vegas, and on the road at tournament venues.

To fast-forward, Tiger won his first regular PGA Tour event, the Las Vegas Invitational, in 1996. Now he has umpteen worldwide wins to his credit, including eight major championships: 1997 Masters, 1999 PGA, 2000 U.S. Open, 2000 British Open, 2000 PGA, 2001 Masters, 2002 Masters, and 2002 U.S. Open.

TIGER GETS HELP FROM HARMON
ON THE MENTAL SIDE

What has been written about in magazines, namely *Golf Digest,* since Tiger started chalking up victories on the professional circuit, is the more advanced-level changes Tiger made to his swing as a pro under the guidance of coach Butch Harmon. Harmon was recently named the number-one teacher in the world by *Golf Digest* magazine. One such change was swinging iron clubs down on a shallower plane to promote clean contact with the ball and prevent the over-the-green "shooter" or "flyer." What has not been written about is how Harmon helped Tiger with the mental side of his game. I'll go into more detail of how the mind plays a role when I analyze such areas as Tiger's preround plan for encouraging peak performance, preshot routine, and shot-making procedures in chapters 4 and 5. But, for now, let's look briefly at how Harmon, who believes "amateurs can do as much to improve the mental side of golf as they can in any other area involving mechanics," helped Tiger shape his game mentally.

1. Harmon showed Tiger videotape of other great players swinging to help him form a clear mental picture of the ideal movements.

2. Harmon showed Tiger video of his own swing so that Tiger could see what he was doing right (or wrong). Having a visual understanding of the ins and outs of your swing and knowing you are swinging well give you confidence. Also, seeing what you are doing wrong when you are not swinging at your best allows you to know exactly what to correct.

3. Harmon passed on to his star student mental strategies he learned from Ben Hogan and his father as a boy. These tips helped Tiger keep thinking about playing golf with a stroke-play mentality rather than a match-play mentality. It's one thing to be aggressive in an amateur event, where you only lose a hole if you score a triple bogey. Medal play, the stroke-play format of the PGA Tour, is different. Tiger needs to score three birdies just to offset a triple bogey and bring his score back to par. The only thing is, par doesn't win you a dime on the professional circuit. Whether your goal is to play the tour or just play a respectable game, the following strategic tips of Hogan's will help you, as they helped Tiger:

a. Plan out your course strategy by looking at the hole backwards—from green to tee, instead of vice versa.

b. Take a little extra time to prepare on the first tee.

c. Play a highly controlled fade off the tee, whenever possible, because this shot is much easier to control than a draw.

d. When hitting an approach shot under pressure, and you're in between clubs, take a more lofted club; e.g., a six iron instead of a five iron. This is the smart strategy because, in a tense course situation, the tendency is to hit the ball longer than normal due to the flow of adrenaline. Also, in this situation, the last thing you want to try to do is take something off the shot. You are better off approaching the shot confidently and swinging harder.

e. Concentrate on hitting fairways and greens.

f. Leave an approach shot into a sloping green on the low side of the hole to set up an easy putt or chip.

g. If you can't attack the hole on your approach shot because of a bad drive, play to your strengths. For example, if you are a better sand player than chipper, consider purposely aiming for a bunker.

h. Swing more slowly in wind. The slower swing helps you maintain good balance and stay in control of the club.

i. Play according to the 4-F philosophy. Make fortitude, faith, focus, and foxiness your on-course priorities.

4. Harmon encouraged Tiger to use his imagination around the green and play inventive shots such as a three-wood chip from the fringe grass.

5. Harmon encouraged Tiger to experiment hitting different shots in practice, so that he stayed stimulated mentally and enhanced his shot-making repertoire.

6. Harmon tuned up Tiger's golf game during a break in Tiger's busy tour schedule. These sessions were all business, with precision being the priority. Harmon knows that the only way Tiger is going to leave the practice tee feeling super-relaxed physically and super-confident mentally is by knowing that his setup and swing mechanics are perfect.

At the start of these tune-up lessons, Harmon liked Tiger to pick out a target, then focus his mental energy on that target when addressing the ball. The more target orientated you are, the more likely you are to swing the club through correctly and propel the ball toward it.

Harmon also preferred that Tiger's practice swing be a true rehearsal of the swing he intended to put on the ball. Only when the practice swing resembles the "real" swing and is not just a casual loosening-up action with the club can you then address the ball confidently. So whenever you make a practice swing, devote 100 percent concentration to that exercise. You'll find the added bonus of doing this is being so tuned in to your body that you will pick up or sense a swing error and be able to correct it on your next practice swing. Better yet, when it comes time to make a "real" swing and actually hit the ball, you'll be better able to employ a mistake-free action.

Harmon also wanted Tiger to know that he was aiming the clubface squarely at the target and setting his feet and body parallel to the target line, simply because this knowledge promotes a positive mental attitude that, in turn, promotes a tension-free, technically sound swing. What helps Tiger set up correctly to a distant target is pointing the club at an interim target spot a few feet in front of the ball and directly in line with an area of fairway or the flagstick he is aiming at. Still, Harmon usually stood a few yards behind the ball to confirm that Tiger was set up in a square address position. He then looked at Tiger's setup from the front view to make sure he was not leaning his body weight too much toward or away from the target. To promote confidence and good tee shots, set your feet slightly wider than shoulder-width apart and balance your weight evenly on the ball of each foot.

Once Tiger set up to the ball, Harmon checked Tiger's grip. He looked for the palms of both hands to be parallel to each other. Both he and Tiger made sure that the right hand was not too far under the grip, in an overly strong position, or else it would take over the downswing and prevent the left hand from playing the lead role in bringing the club into impact. The next thing to be checked was grip pressure. Harmon confirmed that Tiger felt equal pressure in his fingers, about six or seven on a one-to-ten scale.

Tiger's hands are quite small, so he still feels more comfortable using an interlock grip taught to him originally by Rudy Duran. You, on the other hand, may sense that your hands feel more unified and allow you to be more confident about hitting the ball powerfully and accurately by overlapping your right pinky over your left forefinger.

Most of the pros on the PGA Tour, LPGA Tour, and Senior PGA Tour prefer the overlap grip. Ironically, however, Tiger and Jack Nicklaus, two of the greatest golfers ever, prefer the interlock hold. The best advice I can give you is to experiment in practice and determine which grip provides you with the most personal comfort and positive frame of mind.

When Tiger swung, Harmon wanted the club to move along a wide arc. You create one by extending your hands and arms away from the target, so that when the club reaches waist level the wrists are locked and the toe of the club points upward at the sky. At the top, the hands should be extended high, a few inches above the head.

The angle, or plane, of the swing is important, too.

Harmon made sure that Tiger's plane was more upright than flat and that the clubhead never swung far behind his body. An upright swing gives you the best chance of swinging along the target line and through the ball at impact. So it's a good idea to have a friend check that your club never enters the "danger zone," or else you'll find it very difficult to return the clubface to a square impact position.

When checking the downswing, Harmon made sure that Tiger maintained the angle in his right wrist until entering the impact zone, because this is one of the secrets of creating power. Next, he checked that Tiger unhinged the right wrist through impact, because this is one of the secrets of unleashing power.

Harmon told me that when Tiger feels he is making the right swing movements and receives confirmation that he's correct and smoothly coordinating the movement of the club with the movement of the body, he feels good about his chances of playing well in an upcoming competition. This is why Harmon went to great lengths when he analyzed Tiger's technique during breaks in Tiger's schedule. His goal was to make Tiger's swing work as efficiently as possible. Therefore, if Tiger was not satisfied with his ball striking, Harmon usually put things right by making a small adjustment in Tiger's swing or by giving him a simple drill or swing thought to concentrate on. Even if Harmon saw Tiger making more than one swing fault, he almost always gave him just one key to remedy the problems. Because Harmon is such an excellent teacher, that singular key, such as "Let the swing operate from the ground up," usually eliminated the root cause of the major fault, and, with that, other minor faults fell away as easily as dominoes tumbling over.

7. When Tiger was swinging well, Harmon encouraged him to get away to clear his head. Having learned that breaks are good for the brain, Tiger often plays friendly games of golf during his time off, goes fishing, meditates, or simply relaxes at home—goofs off, as they say.

Tiger improved a great deal "studying" under Harmon. Tiger swings more freely than ever before and hits the ball longer and straighter, thanks to Harmon's lessons and paying attention to one particular tip Harmon received from Jack Burke, Jr., and passed on to Tiger. "Swing as if you're hitting the ball into the Pacific Ocean," said Burke. With that leeway, it's no surprise Tiger is so mentally at ease when he sets up to drive.

Thanks to Harmon's help, Tiger's distance control on iron shots is now excellent, too. He's a more inventive shot maker. He's a better short-game player. He sinks more putts. Most of all, he thinks more clearly, rarely making a strategic error, as Jack Nicklaus attests. "Tiger's the smartest player in golf," said Nicklaus, following Tiger's win in the 2001 Memorial at the Nicklaus-designed Muirfield Village course in Columbus, Ohio. Regardless of Tiger's success in tournaments and the stacks of cash he's earned, he takes nothing for granted. That's why he prepares extrahard when it comes time to compete in a major championship.

In the world of professional golf, the four majors—the Masters tournament, U. S. Open Championship, the Open Championship (British), and PGA Championship—are what matter most to professional golfers. So it's venues such as the Augusta National in Augusta, Georgia, where the Masters is played ever year in April, or St. Andrews, the seaside links course in Scotland, where the British Open is often contested, where you can best see the mental-game qualities in Tiger really come out. Tiger gives such weight to each major championship that he works very hard to prepare. It's this solid preparation, described in detail in the next chapter, that allows him to play more confidently and avoid making unforced mental errors.

THINK LIKE TIGER

- Make changes to your swing under the guidance of a qualified golf pro to promote better, more consistent play and allow you to think more positively.
- Think about hitting fairways and greens.
- Use your imagination when planning out short-game shots.
- Practice hitting new shots to stimulate your mind and make yourself more enthusiastic about reaching your goal of lowering your handicap.
- Concentrate on the basic fundamentals that govern the setup and swing to increase your chances of hitting on-target shots.
- Take time off to receive swing tune-ups from your golf instructor.
- When you're swinging well, do something else constructive to escape from golf and clear your head.

4.

ON-COURSE, OFF-COURSE PREP WORK

Tiger's intelligent preround preparation and clearly thought-out preshot routine alleviate mental anxiety and promote peak performance.

PRE-CHAMPIONSHIP PRACTICE ROUND PREPARATION

One chief reason Tiger usually arrives a few days early at a tournament, particularly a major championship, is to assess the course conditions. He carefully considers the depth of the rough, the firmness and speed of the fairways and greens, and the pin placements. He also looks closely at the course design to see if there have been any new features added, such as an extended tee that makes the hole longer or a more expansive area of manicured fringe grass around the green that could change his chipping strategy. Calculating the yardage measurements from the tee to good and bad landing areas, with the help of caddy Steve Williams, is important, too.

To eliminate anxiety and build confidence, it's also important that Tiger know the precise distance from various landing areas in the fairway to certain areas of green where the holes are usually situated (front, middle, and back). Measuring the yardage from the center of the fairway to a landing area short of the green, and from one side of the green to the other, is an additional calculation that must be done before the championship begins. Again, Tiger depends on his caddy, "Stevie," to work hard in this area, but he is known as a perfectionist and good watchdog himself.

The various measurements are put into a miniature memo pad booklet, commonly called a "yardage book." However, these course-reference guides normally contain drawings designating hazards, breaks in greens, out-of-bounds areas, and particularly fast and slow greens. This is why Tiger's caddy carries one in his back pocket. During a tournament, you often will see Tiger looking at this book, confirming a yardage measurement or some other shot-making variable. It's this confirmation that allows him to feel totally confident that the shot he is going to play is the right one.

In preparing for competition, Tiger also looks at the

shape, features, and the yardage of par-four and par-five holes to determine which club is best to hit off the tee: a driver, fairway wood, or long iron. To make this determination, he simply tests out each club, hitting a few balls with each. John Anselmo told me that, during practice rounds, Tiger also hits curving shots with each club to see which works best on a hole and provides him with the strongest sense of confidence: a straight shot, fade, or draw. For the record, Tiger carries a driver and three wood, two iron through pitching wedge, plus fifty-six and sixty-degree wedges, and a putter.

After Tiger hits the ideal shot, he drops several balls down from the spot in the fairway where the ball came to rest. Next, according to Anselmo, he usually hits different approach shots with various clubs and aims for different areas of the greens. His objective: to figure out which club and type of shot allow him to hit the ball closest to the hole while taking the least amount of risk. Because Tiger knows that the hole positions change during each of the four days of a regular PGA Tour event or major championship, he hits shots to four different quadrants of the green.

On par-three holes, Tiger practices hitting golf shots with different clubs to varying pin positions, all the time noting the prevailing wind conditions.

Around the green, Tiger tests out various chipping clubs and different swing techniques to see if the normal "flight-time" and "roll-time" ratios hold true. Normally, for example, a four-iron chip will fly 10 percent of the distance to the hole and roll 90 percent of the distance to the hole. A six iron swung at medium speed using an arms-shoulders stroke will yield 25 percent of flight time to 75 percent of roll time. An eight iron yields 40 percent of flight time, a nine iron 50 percent, a pitching wedge 60 percent, and a sand wedge, which Tiger chips with often, 75 percent.

If the average speed of the green is slow, Tiger will probably play a less lofted club or hood the face of a higher lofted club and play a running shot. If the speed of the average green is fast, Tiger is likely to play a more lofted club, usually a sand wedge, and play a lofted shot.

Being able to play either shot obviously helps Tiger's confidence. Having this shot-making latitude will allow you to play with a more positive attitude, too, so let's review the techniques involved in playing the running chip and the floating chip, golf's versions of the grounder and fly ball.

Running Chip Shot Technique

When playing a chip that spends more time running across the green than flying in the air, Tiger employs an all-arms stroke and swings the clubhead along a flat-bottomed arc. His thinking being, obviously, that the less the clubhead rises from the ground the more solidly it will meet the ball. To help you visualize a "no-wrists" chip stroke, like the one Tiger employs, follow the advice of CBS golf analyst Ken Venturi who says to "imagine that your wrists are in a cast."

When preparing to hit this shot, Tiger positions the ball midway between his feet, setting them about ten inches or less apart. According to John Anselmo, this narrow stance lets Tiger feel closer to the ball, which increases his sense of being in complete control of the stroke, and thus induces added confidence. Tiger also uses an open stance—right foot slightly closer to the target line than the left foot—to give himself a clearer picture of the ball-hole line and to provide ample room for the arms to swing the club through. Tiger's shoulders are square to the target line, which promotes a virtually straight-back and straight-through swing path. His knees are flexed slightly, and his weight is set mostly on the left foot and leg where he keeps it throughout the entire stroke. Guaranteed: If you leave 70 percent of your weight on your left side, you, like Tiger, will feel more stable and thus more mentally sure of yourself.

Tiger also sets the clubface square to the hole and keeps his hands ahead of the ball so that the clubshaft leans slightly toward the hole. You want to maintain this hands-ahead position through impact in order to effectively take loft off the club and accomplish your goal of hitting an extralow running shot.

On the backswing, Tiger keeps his head perfectly still and wrists locked; however, he uses a slight rotation of the knees and hips to enhance the rhythm of the stroke.

On the downswing, Tiger makes a fluid arms swing. Your arms should also be your main mental focal point, because if you concentrate on letting them swing freely through, you'll find that the club reaches impact before you know it and brushes the ball away.

Floating Chip Shot Technique

In playing this type of chip with a sand wedge, as Tiger does, first visualize the ball flying about 75 percent of the distance to the hole.

Tiger plays the ball opposite the left heel in a narrow open stance. He also opens his shoulders by pointing them left of the target line. Additionally, he sets his hands slightly behind the ball and clearly sets the majority of his weight on his right foot. The forward ball position encourages Tiger to stay behind the ball at impact, which is highly critical to lofting the ball into the air. Tiger's open shoulders help him swing the club on an out-to-in path that will help him impart left-to-right cut spin on the ball. Tiger's behind-ball hand position will help him slide the clubface under the ball.

Tiger swings the club back principally with his hands and allows his right wrist to hinge freely so the club moves along an upright arc.

On the downswing, Tiger unhinges his right wrist and swings the club down and under the ball using active hand action to direct the motion. Leaving most of his weight on the right foot helps him slide the clubface under the ball.

WHEN PRACTICING SAND SHOTS, TIGER FEELS THE texture of the sand with his feet so he learns if he will have to take less sand or more sand during competition. If the sand is soupy, he takes less sand; if it's crusty, he takes more sand. There is an alternative to this strategy that allows you to take the same amount of sand for all shots and just requires a change in swing speed. If the sand is hard, reduce your speed; when soft, increase it. Try each approach and determine which gives you more confidence.

On the greens, Tiger practices putts from varying lengths, so that he gets used to the pace and learns to deal with the slopes in the surfaces.

Tiger, like all top pros, makes mental notes of what he learns about the course, while his caddy, Steve Williams, writes down information in their book.

Tiger prepares much like a race driver getting used to the track, learning where to accelerate full out, when to downshift, and when to be cautious. Just as the race driver familiarizes himself with the racecourse, Tiger familiarizes himself with the golf course. The harder Tiger works on his homework, the more confident he becomes.

This prep work is time consuming and requires mental strength to be patient and persevere; however, it is one reason why Tiger looks so confident and physically relaxed on the golf course. If you want to lower your scores, you should also take the time to study your course. Practice until you know the most ideal way to play each hole and preserve strokes. By practicing, you will replace self-doubt with self-confidence, just as Tiger does.

PREPARATION ON THE EVE OF A CHAMPIONSHIP

It's been said that during the week of a tournament, the great Ben Hogan used to bring a blackboard with him to his hotel room. As the story goes, on each of the four nights of the seventy-two-hole major championship, Hogan would take chalk and draw out each hole, one at a time, on the board, and include special markings showing where it was best to hit the ball. He would play the entire hole out in his mind before moving on to the next one, and continue this exercise until completing the full eighteen-hole round in his head.

Although Earl Woods was a tough taskmaster when Tiger was growing up, I have no evidence of his taking things to this extreme. Besides, Earl wanted Tiger to get a good night's sleep during actual competition before playing a championship round of golf. Still, according to Tiger's former caddy Michael "Fluff" Cowan, who now caddies for Jim Furyk, Tiger does think and talk out strategies the night before each round. So I would not be surprised to learn that he falls asleep thinking about the round—of course, in a very positive way.

PREROUND PREPARATION ON THE DAY OF A CHAMPIONSHIP

Hogan, it's been said, also used to give himself plenty of time to get to a championship venue. Typically, he'd drive extraslowly to the course and, once there, do everything at a snail's pace, including tying his shoes very slowly so that he was super-relaxed.

Hogan was so conscious of what affected his game positively that he even paid attention to his clothes. He had no use for "loud" colors or trends. Cotton shirts in conservative colors, tailored and perfectly creased trousers, cashmere sweaters for cool weather, new and shiny black or white leather golf shoes, and a white cap from Cavanaugh raised his level of confidence. I have no evidence to prove Tiger copies Hogan. Nevertheless, during the majors, Tiger is sharply dressed—I suspect because his sartorial splendor makes him feel good mentally.

Like Hogan, Tiger is also quieter during the major

championships and appears to float through the gallery as if in some kind of trance. It's obvious to me that Tiger uses techniques taught to him by Dr. Jay Brunza to click into a zone of intense concentration. I say this because of the glare in his eyes. Also, from the moment he arrives on the practice tee before a round, he's superfocused. Warming up with the shorter clubs first, then working his way to the driver, Tiger is tuned in to the max mentally. He just doesn't hit a ball and rake over another. He carefully watches the flight of the ball and the way it behaves with regard to curve and trajectory.

Tiger concentrates so hard when he practices before a tournament round that I'd bet he sometimes pretends he's playing a particular hole, such as the dogleg left second hole at Augusta National. The same fantasy game will help you. Say your second hole is also a dogleg left. See a right-to-left shot play out in your mind's eye before hitting a practice driver. You'll see: Preshot visualization helps you perform better.

Tiger's serious focus also stays with him when he practices his short game. A serious practice attitude readies you for on-course competition and prevents you from becoming mentally lax. If you watch Tiger hit chip shots and putts, his eyes follow the ball until it stops. You can see that he is making further mental notes of how the ball is going to roll on the greens. The putting surfaces are usually cut down to the bone prior to play and made faster for a major championship, particularly the U.S. Open. Therefore, Tiger must make adjustments. He must make adjustments in the bunkers, too, because sand varies from state to state, country to country.

You can learn a lot from just watching Tiger's preparation at a tournament, and there is no reason why you cannot do the very same things he does. Simply get to the course early and spend time practicing intelligently rather than just beating balls with a driver. That way, when the time comes to tee off, you will be pumped up mentally and ready to do battle on the golf course with all the clubs in your bag.

ON-COURSE PREPARATION:
THE ROUTINE

From the time Tiger arrives on the first tee to the time he hits his final putt, you can see from the serious look on his face that he is working hard mentally. His preshot routine is the same every time and is very precise. Tiger is so mentally in the here-and-now that, if you timed his routine with a stopwatch every single time he set up for a shot, the same exact number of seconds would go by.

When it comes time for Tiger to prepare for a shot, he is like a commercial jet pilot preparing for takeoff by going through a checklist. You, too, should be as methodical as Tiger, because following a preshot routine promotes a positive mind-set and a good shot. Conversely, a haphazard, rushed routine that often varies from one time to the next promotes anxiety and off-line shots.

The next time you watch Tiger play, take note of the steps involved in his preshot routine. Then, the next time you play, follow the ten steps that I have also included here to enable you to be mentally focused in on your target and prepared to swing the club confidently at that target, just like Tiger:

STEP 1: Tiger stands next to his caddy, slowly opening and closing his eyes. In studying Tiger, I'm convinced that other than a means of relaxing, this is a conscious cue used to trigger the preshot routine. Dr. Dick Coop has convinced many top pros that they should use a conscious cue, such as releasing the Velcro on their golf glove or removing, then replacing their cap, to trigger their routine.

Alternatively, Tiger's slow-motion open-shut eye action could also be used to turn on the switch to the subconscious in the same way sports psychologist Dr. Cary Mumford recommends that students use a *release key* to release the golf swing with no conscious effort. Phil Ritson, the renowned golf instructor who coached David Leadbetter in his early days, has spent time with Mumford. Ritson told me that the secret to connecting to the subconscious is to use a simple verbal trigger or key that has nothing to do with golf, such as "Merry Christmas." Apparently, when you say the release key aloud, you can't think of anything else.

Ritson, in a book I worked with him on called *Golf Your Way,* says:

> The release key forces your mind to focus on the present moment only, rather than on past bad shots or future holes that require a superprecise shot and stir anxiety in the head. In a sense, I guess developing a release key for your swing is something like the development of the mantra that is used by practitioners of many Eastern religious philosophies. This mantra is their focus on which they strive to develop a heightened awareness. Although the awareness you seek is not quite as far reaching as that of the Eastern mystic, the principle involved is very much the same. You, too, are increasing your awareness of the present moment by repeating your release key as you swing.

Tiger's "eye drill," whether conscious or unconscious, lets everything just happen on the course. Tiger doesn't get hung up on technique, and that is very advantageous when you are playing in a pressure-filled major championship.

STEP 2: After deliberating with his caddy, Tiger chooses a club. Only if you select the right club, based on yardage, lie, and course conditions, will you feel confident and make a good swing.

Tiger's preparation before the tournament is thorough, so when he plays in competition he pretty much knows which club he is going to hit from the tee or fairway; however, sometimes the wind direction and strength are much different in play than they were in practice. Therefore, Tiger has to make adjustments, such as using a two iron off the tee when playing into a strong wind on a short par-four hole and hitting a piercing shot that cheats the wind. In hitting an approach shot into wind, Tiger plays a stronger club, and when the wind is behind him, a weaker club.

If Tiger's tee-shot game does not go as planned, he also has to make some changes when playing out of rough. Most often, he takes less club to allow for the ball flying farther due to blades of grass or moisture inevitably intervening between the ball and the clubface at impact.

STEP 3: Standing a few yards behind the ball, Tiger picks out a target, either to the right of an area of fairway or the flagstick to allow for a right-to-left draw shot or left of these targets to allow for a left-to-right fade.

The choice Tiger makes has to do with the hole's design and the conditions. For example, when hitting a tee shot on the hole that doglegs left, he'll normally hit his bread-and-butter draw.

On days when his distance control is really good, he'll aim straight at the flag on approach shots; however, if it's a little off or bunkers and water hazards are situated in dangerous places right of the green, he'll aim left and fade the ball into the hole.

STEP 4: Tiger stares at the target, surely to form a visual picture in his mind of the ball flying on a specific line toward its final target.

It's obvious that Buddhist meditation has helped Tiger's concentration. According to John Anselmo, Tiger is better able to maintain his focus of attention on the hole or flagstick better than most pros.

STEP 5: Tiger makes a practice swing while looking at the target. When rehearsing the swing, make sure you stare at the target, too, and concentrate on feeling the action, because this will make you more confident and likely to repeat a good action when it comes time to make a real swing. Staring at the target will also make you more apt to swing through the ball and not at the ball.

If you have trouble looking at a distant target, this tip from teaching guru and good friend Jim McLean should help: "Stand behind your ball, then pick an aiming point about ten feet ahead of the ball that is a suspended window at the height you desire. This window image will reduce your peripheral sight and help you concentrate on the swing."

STEP 6: Tiger steps into the ball from the side, right foot first, and stares at the target so intently that he appears as if he is looking down the sight of a rifle.

STEP 7: Tiger usually sets the clubhead behind the ball, so its face is perpendicular to his target.

STEP 8: Tiger jockeys his left foot into position. In establishing the proper stance, Tiger's left foot points outward while the right one is pretty much perpendicular to the target line. The width of his stance is slightly wider than shoulder width when playing drives and narrows progressively as the clubs get shorter.

The position of the feet may seem incidental, but the proper stance is a vital link to being comfortable and confident over the ball. Copying Tiger's stance will give you a firm base to coil against and allow you to clear your hips freely on the downswing. The clearing action of the hips opens up a clear passageway for the hands and arms to swing the club into the ball. So it is vital to making solid and square clubface-to-ball contact at impact.

STEP 9: Tiger glances at an interim target spot in line with the main target and a few feet in front of the ball, then refocuses on his main target. He looks back down at the ball, then at the main target a couple of times. This same peek-a-boo procedure will help you feel the distance and line up correctly, boosting your confidence.

STEP 10: Tiger triggers the swing by swinging his arms and the club away together.

COURSE PREPARATION

Earl Woods, Rudy Duran, John Anselmo, and Butch Harmon also taught Tiger how to strengthen his mental game by following a set of sophisticated rules that go beyond the basic steps included in the aforementioned routine. Study these rules, because they will make you a more confident golfer and allow you to cut strokes off your score.

Rule #1: Be Mentally Confident About Your Swing

To fight off any anxiety about making a good swing, particularly on the first tee, copy Tiger. Make a smooth (not slow) practice swing until you feel the sensations of the clubhead reaching the top and swishing through impact. If you are unable to employ the right actions the first time, take a couple of deep breaths, or open and close your eyes slowly, as Tiger does, to induce a relaxed state of mind. Next, make a couple more swings until you find the one that you want to match when it comes time to hit the ball. Once you discover your ideal swing, set up to the ball. As you will discover, you will feel confident and experience no first-tee jitters.

Rule #2: Be Positive About the Shot
You Are About to Hit

All Tiger's coaches, including his former psychologist, Dr. Jay Brunza, have taught Tiger the value of putting a positive thought into his mind when standing over a shot. You should, too. Whatever shot you are about to hit, pick a target and say to yourself: "That's where I'm going to hit the ball. The more positive you are about hitting your target and the clearer your mental image of the ball flying toward it, the better the chance that you will succeed.

"Visualization enables us to conjure up confidence, boosting alignments or scenarios that assist us in freeing our minds from doubt, anxiety, or other inhibiting negative thoughts," says Larry Miller, golf teacher, spiritual coach, and author of *Golfing in the Zone.*

You'll also find it easier to stay positive if you favor your natural shot or the one you bring to the course on a given day. If you usually hit a fade, don't try to hit a draw. If on the practice tee before the round you notice that you are hitting a controlled draw, however, don't try to switch back to a fade. Take the new draw shot with you to the course, as long as you can repeat it over and over.

Rule #3: Think About Swinging the Club to Alleviate Anxiety About Hitting the Ball

"Trust allows you to think straight, and you must trust that the ball will be hit," says Timothy Gallwey, the author of *The Inner Game of Golf*.

Something Duran impressed upon Tiger, from the day he started taking lessons at age four, was to stand to the ball and realize that his short-term goal was to imagine himself swinging the club and not hitting the ball.

The old adages "The ball gets in the way of a good swing" and "Swing the force; don't force the swing" certainly apply. Drum these statements into your head when taking your address. Also, remember this: If you set up to the ball properly, make a timed takeaway action, turn your body on the backswing, and uncoil your hips on the downswing, the swing will take care of hitting the ball— automatically.

Rule #4: Don't Focus on Quick Swing Fixes; Focus on What You Know Works

One of the most common mistakes amateur golfers make is analyzing their swing during the round, usually in between shots. They look for a new and quick way to fix a fault, such as turning the clubface inward to correct a slice.

If you run into a problem during a round, forget about what's wrong and focus your attention on what to do right. That's what Tiger has been trained to do. When standing over the ball, revert back to the basics, concentrating on a good grip, square setup, smooth backswing, and full follow-through rather than searching for a quick fix. This is the only true shortcut to hitting good shots and restoring your confidence.

If for some reason you still experience trouble, spend time on the practice tee after the round, ideally with your instructor, to pinpoint your faults and correct them. Keep practicing until you recapture that "I got it" feeling.

Rule #5: Concentrate on Performance, Not Score

To alleviate tension and play with positive energy, focus on the shot at hand. After grinding hard mentally to hit a good tee shot, Tiger walks to the ball to play his next shot. Once he reaches the ball, he starts focusing his attention on what he will do next. This entails looking at the hazards near the green, the slopes in the putting surface, and the position of the pin to get a jump start on the right strategy.

Give each shot full concentration, and the good scores will come.

Rule #6: Stay in Control of Your Emotions

Tiger is much more levelheaded than he used to be, learning that it is best to go with the flow and not overreact to a bad shot or get superexcited over a good shot. "No matter what happens with any shot you hit, accept it," says performance consultant to the pros Dr. Bob Rotella, author of *Golf Is Not a Game of Perfect.*

Drastic emotional swings negatively affect your concentration and thus hinder the way you play the upcoming shot. If you overreact to a bad shot and hold on to that mental baggage, chances are you will make a faulty fast swing and hit a bad next shot. If you overreact to a good shot, the tendency is to become lackadaisical on the next shot and hit it left or right of target.

According to the Buddhist religion, when you gain wisdom you learn not to expect anything, good or bad— which is precisely how Tiger's mother taught him to be patient on the course. Furthermore, by disciplining yourself to let go like Tiger and Buddhist Zen masters, you will alleviate pressure, not just deal with it, and make fewer unforced errors.

THINK LIKE TIGER

- Know your course so well that you can visualize any hole when planning your strategies.
- Follow the flight of the ball until it comes to rest, then make mental notes of how it behaved in the air and on the ground. This tracking procedure will make you a more focused player and allow you to receive important shot-making feedback.

- Hit various shots with various clubs in practice rounds to determine the club-shape of shot combinations that give you the most confidence and best results.
- The quicker you learn to follow a set preshot routine, one that becomes automatic, the more likely you are to let go and allow the subconscious mind to control the swinging action.
- Make a smooth practice swing, one that matches the one you intend to use when hitting the ball, so when it comes time to swing you are more confident mentally.
- Put a positive thought in your mind before you swing, such as "I'm going to hit the center of the fairway," to help promote a tension-free swing.
- Concentrate on swinging the force, not forcing the swing, to help eliminate anxiety.
- Think good performance, not score, and good scores will come.
- Stay levelheaded no matter whether you score a birdie or a double bogey on a hole.

5.

MENTAL MASTERY

Simple mental images given to Tiger by top teachers
help him put the basic fundamentals into action
and hit tee-to-green supershots.

I HAVE WRITTEN BOOKS WITH QUITE A FEW PGA
Tour pros, including multiple major winners Seve Ballesteros and Sandy Lyle, as well as top teachers, most notably
John Anselmo and Butch Harmon. The one common thread
among these great golf champions and instructors regarding shot-making is believing that a vital link to good play is
using a visual key to promote a smooth, technically sound
swing. For example, on long pitch-and-run shots, Ballesteros, who is still a great short-game player, promotes lively
lower-body action by trying to clash a pair of imaginary mu-

sical cymbals attached to the inside of each knee. When hitting medium irons, Lyle told me he imagines taking a bacon strip–type divot rather than a pork-chop divot to promote a cleanly hit shot instead of a fat shot. Anselmo likes students to imagine they are swinging a range ball basket instead of a club so that they relax physically and take their minds off hitting at the ball. Harmon often instructs students to think of moving an imaginary triangle formed by the arms and shoulders to help them make fluid putting and chipping strokes.

I have just given you four examples of how professional golfers and golf instructors use the mind to their advantage. The fact is, unlike most high-handicap players who just get up and hit the ball, all golf instructors teach students to use mental imagery to help them employ better swings and execute better golf shots. And I have observed during my sixteen-year stint as senior instruction editor for *Golf* magazine that every top pro on the PGA Tour—from Paul Azinger to Tiger Woods—depends on the mind to enhance his performance on the golf course.

Tiger is sure lucky to have had teachers who believe in keeping things simple. From tee to green, Tiger makes the game look easy. According to Anselmo, this is because Tiger does not allow himself to let a zillion different swing thoughts enter his head and get him tied up mentally. Neither should you. One solid mental image will help you get the job done.

What follows are instructions for playing a variety of shots that Tiger actually played on his way to victory in the major championships and other prestigious professional events. In presenting these, I include unique physical moves employed by Tiger and tell you how to match them. I also tell you how to use your imagination and rely on mental imagery, as Tiger does when hitting shots. Because I can't possibly read this shot-making virtuoso's mind, my information is based on my own expertise as a swing analyst and former golf instructor, and what I learned from Tiger's teachers about the link between using one's imagination and good shot-making.

No matter what your handicap, it is good idea to have a clear understanding of the basic fundamentals, but especially Tiger's basic moves, because they are something special. As for the mental images, try them out and see how they work, never being afraid to invent one of your own to help you play a particular shot.

TRACKING TIGER'S MIND-GOLF PERFORMANCE IN MAJOR CHAMPIONSHIPS

Sweeping Draw

When you hit this shot, the ball starts down the right side of the fairway, turns gently left in the air, touches down essentially in the center of the fairway, takes a couple of big bounces, then runs an extra twenty-five to fifty yards due to the overspin imparted to it. The firmer the fairway, the more the ball runs.

Tiger played the sweeping draw often in all three Masters championships he won, in 1997, 2001, and 2002 at the Augusta National Golf Club in Augusta, Georgia. The reason is that many holes on the course, such as numbers ten and twelve, curve or dogleg left. Cutting the dogleg effectively shortens the hole and gives you the advantage of hitting a more lofted club into the green. Chances are, you will never hit the ball as far as Tiger, but you will feel really good if you know how to cut the corner of dogleg left holes on your home "track."

TIGER MOVES—HOW TO MATCH THEM: Tee the ball up slightly higher than normal (almost entire ball atop the clubface), take a strong grip (Vs formed by thumbs and forefingers point up at right shoulder), and set your right foot a few inches farther away from the target line (in a closed position). These three setup elements will promote a flat backswing that, in turn, allows your hands and fore-arms to rotate more vigorously in a counterclockwise direc-tion in the hit zone. As a result, the clubface closes slightly at impact, and overspin is imparted to the ball.

No matter what shot he plays, Tiger seems to do some-thing extraordinary, like opening his shoulders (aiming them left of target) to play the superhigh sweeping draw. This setup position will allow you to move more freely through the impact zone and generate high club-head speed. More speed means more distance, provided that you square the clubface to the ball at impact.

Tiger also sets his hands behind the ball slightly. Copy his hand position, and you'll find it easier to hit the golf ball powerfully on the upswing.

To allow for the draw, aim the clubface at the area of fairway down the right side. This is the spot you should stare at, and see yourself hitting before you swing, in order to send a positive message to your brain.

In swinging back, extend the club back low to the ground and along the target line for about twelve inches, then straight back past your body. As soon as the club's shaft parallels the ground at waist level, hinge your wrists and swing up to the top while turning your shoulders and hips clockwise. By extending the club back, you create a power-ful arc of swing, and by turning the shoulders more than the hips you create valuable added torque in the swing.

Coming down, shift your weight to your left foot and leg, then rotate your hips counterclockwise to open up a passageway for your hands and arms to swing the club down into the ball and then through it.

Use Your Imagination: *Visualize a door swinging open, then closing, just as Earl Woods told Tiger when he was a boy. This mental image will allow you to swing on the proper flat plane, come into impact with the toe of the club leading the heel, and impart overspin to the ball virtually automatically.*

Rocket Fade

This is a shot that flies high and slightly left of target, then drifts back toward it. The fade is the ideal shot to hit on dogleg right holes because, essentially, it allows you to shorten the hole by cutting the corner of the dogleg and play a medium or short iron into the green. These types of clubs are much easier to control than low-lofted irons, mainly because they are shorter in length and more lofted. The rocket fade also can be used on approach shots to bend the ball around a corner.

The most memorable rocket fade tee shot I saw Tiger hit was on the par-four tenth hole at St. Andrews in Scotland, during the final round of the 2000 British Open. The ball seemed to fly into the stratosphere, and when it came down it landed on the green. Two putts later, Tiger scored a birdie and pulled away from his nearest rival, David Duval.

Another time, on the seventh hole of the final round of the 1999 PGA Championship at Medinah Country Club in Medinah, Illinois, it was another type of rocket fade shot hit by Tiger that impressed me. After hitting his tee shot on the 588-yard par-five hole, Tiger faced a 237-yard shot around a corner. What did he do? He hit a powerful left-right rocket fade shot around the trees and onto the green. He took two putts for a birdie, then went on to win the coveted title from Spanish sensation, Sergio Garcia.

TIGER MOVES—HOW TO MATCH THEM: Hold the club with a weak grip by moving both hands slightly toward the target, so that the Vs formed by your thumbs and forefingers point up at your chin. Take an open stance by placing your right foot a few inches closer to the target line than your left. Stand taller to the ball than normal to encourage an upright swing plane. Play the ball forward in the stance, even off the left instep if that allows you to feel more confident about hitting the ball on the upswing.

Swing the club back outside the target line and stop at the three-quarter point.

On the downswing, swing across the ball. It's really important that you turn your right hand under your left through impact to promote an upswing hit and added loft.

To ensure that the ball fades, you must hold on a little longer with the left hand so that you release the club a split second later.

Use Your Imagination: *Imagine your left hand as super-hard Bethlehem Steel. That's what Butch Harmon taught Tiger to do to encourage a delayed-release action, with a firm left hand and a slightly open club-face position at impact.*

Two-Iron Stinger

This is a dead straight low piercing shot that is ideal when playing a supernarrow hole featuring fast-running fairways. In Tiger's case, it came in handy at the 2000 U.S. Open, the 2000 Tournament Players Championship, the 2000 PGA, and the 2001 World Golf Championship NEC Invitational. Respectively, these championships were contested at the following courses: Pebble Beach Golf Links in Pebble Beach, California; TPC at Sawgrass in Ponte Vedra Beach, Florida; Valhalla Golf Club in Louisville, Kentucky; and Firestone Country Club in Akron, Ohio.

Had Tiger just gotten up on every par-four and par-five hole and smacked the driver, as he sometimes did as an amateur and young pro, he probably would never have won these championships.

TIGER MOVES—HOW TO MATCH THEM: Grip the club normally, using a neutral hold. Check that the Vs formed by your thumbs and forefingers point up at a spot midway between your chin and right shoulder.

Play the ball opposite a point about two inches behind your left heel. Set up square to the ball, with your feet, knees, hips, and shoulders aligned parallel to the target line and the club perpendicular to the target. Balance your weight evenly on the ball of each foot. Keep your hands in line with the ball.

Swing the club back along a wide arc, then up to the three-quarter point, keeping wrist action to a minimum. You also want the back of the left hand and left wrist to line up and remain flat to ensure a square club-face position at the top.

On the downswing, shift your weight to your left foot, then practically simultaneously slide your hips laterally. Next, rotate your hips counterclockwise to give yourself room to return the clubface squarely to the ball.

Use Your Imagination: *Visualize Ben Hogan swinging down into impact using powerful hip action. Maybe the reason Tiger's is so good when he's "on" is that teacher Butch Harmon showed him films of Hogan swinging and probably told him the same story he told me.*

"My dad had a film that proved that Mr. Hogan had the best downswing action of all time," said Harmon when we worked together on *The Four Cornerstones of Winning Golf*. "Funnily enough, Mr. Hogan's hip slide during the downswing was highlighted by the fact that, in the film, there was a man on the beach behind him who appeared just to the left of Ben's left hip. At the top of Ben's backswing, you could see the guy, but at impact, his left hip moved so far laterally that the guy was blocked out of the picture."

Forming an image of Hogan swinging down in your mind before you swing will help you make the right moves and hit the "stinger" powerfully and accurately.

Tailoring the Tip: The best way to practice this shot is to swing the club into an old rubber tire. Whether you use a tire or feel more comfortable hitting into a softer Impact Bag available in pro shops, practicing this drill will encourage you to accelerate the left hand and arm so that the shot you hit "burns rubber."

Medium Iron Stop-Shot

This is a shot that flies extrahigh and lands extrasoftly on the green, so it's ideal when playing out of light rough and the green you're hitting to is small and firm.

Tiger hit this shot with a seven iron on the par-five sixth hole at Pebble Beach, during the 2000 U.S. Open Championship at Pebble Beach Golf Links in Pebble Beach, California. The ball flew all the way to the green. Tiger took two putts, scoring a birdie on his way to victory.

TIGER MOVES—HOW TO MATCH THEM: Play the ball in the middle of your stance. Take one club more than normal (e.g., a five iron rather than a six iron) and lay the clubface open when setting up. Put 60 percent of your weight on your right foot. Make sure that your left arm is extended. More important, set your left hip higher than your right.

Swing the club back on a steep plane, leaving the majority of your weight on your right foot and leg.

Coming down, keep your weight on your right side and swing the club under the ball with the clubface facing the sky.

Use Your Imagination: *Imagine swinging a range ball basket back and through. Anselmo used to have Tiger do this when he first came for lessons. In watching him execute this shot at "Pebble," I wouldn't be surprised if he used this image to take the pressure off and depended on a fluid arm-swing action to execute the shot.*

Fairway Bunker Cut

This is a shot that, like a Lear jet taking off, rises into the air extrafast. The reason it is such a highly controlled shot is because it flies very high and only moves slightly from left to right in the air. The other plus factor of playing this approach shot over a straight shot or draw is that the ball spins gently to the right upon landing. So it's ideal if you want to land the ball on the "fat" side of the green, left of the hole, and spin it down a slope toward the hole.

Tiger played the high cut from a fairway bunker on the seventy-second hole of the 2000 Canadian Open. He hit this shot from 218 yards out from the green with a six iron. Talk about making things happen! Tiger sailed the ball over water toward the flag, to birdie the hole and beat New Zealander Grant Waite by one stroke.

TIGER MOVES—HOW TO MATCH THEM: Hold the club with a firm left-hand grip and play the ball opposite your left heel. Position your hands behind the ball to promote a clean hit on the upswing. Take one more club than normal (e.g., a six iron instead of a seven iron) to compensate for the added height and left-to-right flight pattern of the ball.

Open the clubface according to how much cut spin you want to impart to the ball. The more you want the ball to drift right and spin once it hits the green, the more you should open the clubface. In short, aim the clubface where you want the ball to complete its flight, and your feet and body along the line you want the ball to start its flight.

To set yourself up to make a Tiger-type swing, you must also assume a square stance, being sure to turn your left foot a little outward and point the toe end of your right foot perpendicular to the target line. Setting your feet down in the sand in this manner will allow you to employ a powerful upright backswing and more easily clear your left side during the downswing. This hip clearance gives the arms and hands ample room to swing the club freely along the target line through impact.

Because this is virtually a total hands and arms shot, wiggle your feet into the sand quite deeply, but not so much that you feel you're stuck.

On the backswing, set the club early on an upright arc and stop when it reaches the three-quarter point.

On the downswing, uncock your right wrist earlier than normal, so you accelerate the club into impact. You'll make contact early, with a slightly open clubface, ensuring a controlled cut shot.

Use Your Imagination: *Practice swinging on grass before stepping into the bunker, as Harmon students are instructed to do when they take a playing lesson with him. Carry the image of the grass into the sand, as this will allow you to stay positive and relax in a tense course situation. Tiger's been fortunate to have had teachers who stress the importance of mental imagery.*

Low Short-Iron Spinner

This is a relatively low shot that lands on the green with exaggerated right-to-left spin. The ball bounces left, then trickles toward the hole.

Tiger played this shot on the eleventh hole during the final round of the 2001 Masters. He worked the ball away from a water hazard located on the left side of the green and well right of the hole that on that day was situated on the left side of the putting surface. The ball landed on the green, bounced gently to the left, then trickled close to the hole. Tiger scored a birdie and went on to win the green jacket, presented each year to the winner of this prestigious event.

TIGER MOVES—HOW TO MATCH THEM: In setting up to hit this shot, play the ball in the middle of your stance. Aim your body a little to the right—where you want the ball to start its flight—and aim the clubface at your final target.

Make a smooth, rounded backswing. Use very little wrist action and control the swing with your arms.

Swing the clubhead through the ball longer than normal so that you sweep the ball cleanly off the turf and hardly take a divot.

Use Your Imagination: *Conjure up a mental image that relaxes you physically and enables you to employ a rhythmic swing. For example, as you set up, picture yourself hitting the ball and watching it until it stops rolling, as teacher Rudy Duran used to have Tiger actually do during practice. This image will encourage you to stay down with the shot and, in turn, employ good balance during the swing.*

Sand Splash

This is a unique shot that floats over the bunker's lip, flies from left to right, lands softly, spins right, then rolls gently toward the hole.

Tiger hit this shot from about thirty feet on the seventy-first hole of the 2000 U.S. Open at Pebble Beach. The ball landed within inches of the hole, shocking NBC golf commentators Roger Maltby and Gary Koch. He tapped the ball in for par and went on to victory.

TIGER MOVES—HOW TO MATCH THEM: Grip the club lightly to promote lively hand action and choke down on it to compensate for digging your feet more deeply into the sand. Position the ball opposite your left heel, so you can more easily contact the sand at the bottom of the swing's arc, with the club moving fluidly through it. For best results, stand open like Tiger, with your feet, knees, hips, and shoulders aiming well left of the hole. Open the clubface so its leading edge points at the hole.

Swing the club back outside the target line on an upright plane, while allowing the wrists to hinge freely.

On the downswing, swing the club along the line of your feet and body, turn your right hand under the left to help you keep the clubface open through impact, and unhinge your right wrist so that you can snap the bounce of the club into the sand behind the ball.

Use Your Imagination: *Imagine a four-inch ruler stretching back from behind the ball. The number 1 is closest to the hole, the number 4 farther away. Slap the number 4 with the bounce of the sand wedge, so that the club digs down under the ball and slides through the sand under it. The rest is history. Butch Harmon was taught how to play bunker shots by his father, and he passed on his tips to Tiger.*

Superlob

This is a shot played near the green, and it's ideal when hitting to a tight pin on a sloping green. It's ideal, too, when the ball is sitting down in spongy grass and you have to stop it quickly on the green. Many of today's greens are very undulating. Therefore, a pitch-and-run shot often rolls past the hole and sometimes over the green. The superlob works far better particularly when hitting over a bunker and there's very little green to work with or when the hole is cut at the base of a slope in the green.

Tiger played this shot en route to victory on hole number eight in the last round of the 2001 Masters. He floated the ball up about eight feet from the hole and made the birdie putt.

TIGER MOVES—HOW TO MATCH THEM: The most important setup key is laying the clubface back more at address to increase its natural loft. Tiger plays the superlob with a sand wedge and opens the clubface dramatically.

However, a sixty-degree wedge is also ideal for playing this shot, especially because you can just let its natural loft work for you.

On the backswing, allow your left wrist to cup or bend inward in a slightly concave position. This is a wrist position Tiger has worked to change in the full swing, but not when playing the lob. The reason is that the cupped left wrist opens the clubface, so that the sand wedge's normal fifty-five degrees of loft increase to about seventy degrees. The other advantage of cupping the left wrist is that it prevents you from closing the clubface at impact and hitting that low pitch-and-run shot I talked about earlier. Knowing this before you swing will make you think more positively about executing the shot.

Another basic backswing move involves the right wrist. Let it hinge freely, because this early-set action will help you make a full swing like Tiger's. It will also allow you to better feel the clubhead, so that you will swing the club at the proper speed and hit the ball the correct distance.

On the downswing, think of rotating your hips counterclockwise while maintaining the same cupped and hinged positions of the wrists. Preserving these two wrist positions is Tiger's physical secret link to success, because it allows him to maintain the loft of the club in the impact zone and lob the ball toward a tight pin set on a plateau area of the green and stop it next to the hole.

In hitting this shot, it's also critical that you keep rotating the hips in the hitting area, because this action helps you accelerate the club under the ball. The faster you rotate the hips, the higher the lob shot will fly and the softer it will land next to the hole.

Use Your Imagination: *When Earl Woods trained the youthful Tiger, he had him hit short shots into a bucket set out at the perfect landing spot short of the hole. Retain this in-the-bucket image when you play, as it will help you propel the ball the proper distance. Parents take heed: As Earl said in his popular book,* Training a Tiger, *"It's important to convey to your child the importance of visualizing a spot where he or she wants the ball to land."*

Three-Wood Chip Out

This is the perfect play when the ball rests in the heavier cut of fringe grass near the green and you are about thirty feet away from the hole. The three-wood is a better club to use than the sand wedge because it allows you to make a relatively level stroke and pop the ball up onto the green. A sand wedge requires a sharp hit on the descent, so often the ball flies fast off the clubface and finishes well by the hole.

Tiger has played this shot en route to winning many championships around the world and has actually started a trend. More and more PGA Tour pros are hitting this shot nowadays, rather than using a sand wedge as they did previously.

TIGER MOVES—HOW TO MATCH THEM: Set up slightly open to give yourself a better view of the line to the hole and provide added freedom for your arms and hands to swing the club. Balance your weight evenly on the balls of your feet and play the ball opposite your left heel.

If the lie is clean, swing the club back and through using a firm-wristed pendulum-type stroke action, and keep your head still. The loft of the three-wood will lift the ball up over the fringe and roll it like a putt, so don't feel you have to lift the ball up.

Tailoring the Tip: If the ball is sitting down in the grass, set your hands well ahead of it, hinge your right wrist on the backswing, and unhinge it coming down. This technique will allow you to hit down ever so slightly and lift the ball gently over the fringe grass.

Use Your Imagination: *Imagine that your arms and shoulders form a triangle. Keep that triangle intact by maintaining firm wrists, as Harmon taught Tiger, and you will hit a good shot.*

Superslider

This is a long downhill putt that curves left to right on a sloping green.

Tiger played this shot on the seventeenth hole during the final round of the 2001 Tournament Players Championship, considered by the pros to be the "Fifth Major." He rolled the ball from the back of the green to practically the front of the green, into the cup.

TIGER MOVES—HOW TO MATCH THEM: Play the ball more forward in a square stance, with your body and the clubface aimed left of the hole. The more you figure the ball will break, the farther left you should aim. This setup position will ensure that you start the ball rolling on the high side of the hole. Ideally, as the ball nears the hole, it will fall gently toward the cup.

Make a slightly slower arms-and-shoulders stroke and keep the putter low to the ground on the backswing and downswing.

Use Your Imagination: *Imagine a second ball at the crest of the break. If you hit that ball, you're likely to roll the real ball into the hole, as Harmon tells his students.*

Short Roller

This is a pressure putt, inside the ten-foot range, that rolls so smoothly off the putter that it holds its line. The best short roller I saw Tiger hit was on the final hole of the 2000 PGA Championship at Kentucky's Valhalla Golf Club. It was so great it's worth reliving.

The scene is the seventy-second hole. Tiger Woods is standing over an eight-foot putt that could dramatically change the history of the game—at least, if he knocks the ball into the hole. If he misses, he will lose his chance to become the first golfer ever to win the U.S. Open, British Open, and PGA championships in one year, and the first player since the legendary Ben Hogan to win three majors in one year. (In 1953, Hogan won the Masters, U.S. Open, and British Open.)

What's more, if Tiger misses, he will be remembered as being beaten by Bob May, a little-known pro from California who finished off a day of spectacular golf by doing the unthinkable: sinking a thirty-foot birdie putt from the back of the green. The bottom line: Tiger must make the putt to tie May and force a three-hole playoff and keep the record books open.

The situation at Kentucky's Valhalla Golf Club was similar to a world-champion boxer leading a bout over an underdog, then getting hit by a hard uppercut in the fifteenth round. You would have thought that Tiger was finished after May sank the miracle putt. After all, in these situations, it's tough to stand your ground and compose yourself. Suddenly, all these demons of self-doubt enter the mind and you want to scream "Help!" But you know only too well that golf is an individual sport. You are alone. Only you can save the day—or fail.

Where others experience a racing heartbeat and sweaty palms, and succumb to pressure, Tiger thrives on high drama. He likes to test his mental strength against all comers. The more pressure, the better. And that is exactly why he calmly stood over that final putt and knocked it right in the hole to force a playoff. A calm mind and the ability to stay in control in the heat of battle are two reasons he holed that putt. They are also the reasons that, in the playoff with May, he stiffed a bunker shot on the third and final hole of the playoff. This shot set up a winning tap-in birdie putt that changed golf history when it found the bottom of the cup.

TIGER MOVES—HOW TO MATCH THEM: Set up with the ball played opposite a point about two inches behind the left heel, which is the lowest point in the stroke. Position your eyes directly over it. Butch Harmon monitored Tiger's putting setup often, checking to see that he maintained the eyes-over-ball position, knowing that it helps promote an on-line stroke. Additionally, check that your hands line up with the ball, because this position promotes a level back-and-through stroke.

Generally, Tiger sets his feet, knees, hips, and shoulders parallel to the target line to promote the best possible on-line stroke. However, to give himself a clearer view of an awkward uphill putt, or when putting a left-to-right breaking putt, Tiger sets his body slightly left of the target line, in an "open" position. In aligning the putter face, he always sets it down squarely behind the ball, with its sweet spot pointing at the hole.

On both the backswing and downswing, Tiger concentrates on keeping his head perfectly still so his balance is maintained. He also concentrates on swinging the putter low to the ground, in a more streamlined fashion, since this is a secret to achieving a pure roll of ball across green.

Use Your Imagination: *To encourage a steady head position and pure on-line stroke, Harmon told Tiger to imagine his head being held still, which is what they worked on in practice. The same imagery will help you sink more putts.*

THINK LIKE TIGER

- When hitting the sweeping draw shot, visualize a door opening to help you swing the club back on an inside path.
- When hitting the rocket fade, imagine that your left hand is made of steel to help you keep the clubface open slightly through impact, as Harmon taught Tiger to do.
- When hitting the two-iron stinger, visualize Ben Hogan's fluid hip action before you swing.
- When playing the medium-iron stop shot, imagine swinging a range ball basket.
- When playing a fairway bunker cut, think of hitting an iron off grass to take the pressure off.
- When setting up for a low, short-iron spinner, imagine yourself hitting a shot and following the ball until it stops rolling.
- When playing the sand splash, imagine a four-inch

ruler stretching back from behind the ball. The number 1 is closest to the ball. The idea is to slap the number 4 on the imaginary ruler with the bounce of the sand wedge so that you splash the ball out of the bunker.

• When playing the superlob, imagine there is a bucket on your ideal landing spot.

• When hitting a three-wood chip out of a relatively good lie in fringe grass, imagine that your arms and shoulders form a triangle.

• When hitting a superslider, imagine a second ball at the crest of the break. Now, go ahead and hit it with the real ball.

• When hitting a short roller, imagine your head being held still so that you employ a steady stroke.

6.

MENTAL CHALLENGES

Reviewing a round of golf in your head, pinpointing
your swing errors, then using mental buzz phrases
to correct your problems will put your game
back on track—Tiger *style!*

A S GOOD A GOLFER AS TIGER WOODS IS, HE'S NOT
always going to play A-game golf. If Tiger didn't realize this before winning four major championships in a
row, the last the 2001 Masters, he sure realized it after finishing seven strokes behind winner Retief Goosen in the
2001 U.S. Open, nine strokes behind 2001 British Open
winner David Duval, and fourteen strokes behind 2001
PGA champion David Toms.

In these championships, Tiger didn't look at all like the
same old supertalented golfer. And why should he? The golf
press expects this young superstar to win every week, and

that just isn't fair. After doing what no other golfer had done, and probably never will again—holding four major championship trophies at one time—he was expected to carry on as always, forever winning. Well, that was not to be.

Michael Jordan, the basketball legend, has helped Tiger learn how to deal with distractions. Still, it was obvious that, during the last three majors of the 2001 golf season, Tiger was distracted. And, by the look on his face, mentally exhausted, too. I imagine that hounding press and exchanging rest for much too much preparatory work in practice hurt Tiger. His body language, marked by a somewhat sluggish walk and, at times, hunched-over shoulders, proved he had overprepared and was tired both mentally and physically. Frankly, Tiger looked like a prizefighter who had worked too hard to make the weight or a baseball pitcher who had thrown too many warm-up pitches before a World Series game. Before each major, Tiger overpracticed—hit too many practice balls in an attempt to perfect an already good swing. His strategy backfired, as will yours if you don't know how to draw the line between intelligent preparatory work, discussed in chapter 4, and working too hard beating balls on the range and overanalyzing your swing technique. Your lesson: When it comes to your swing, the old adage "If it ain't broke, don't fix it" certainly applies.

It's also difficult to play good golf when you're not with it, particularly since these poor conditions of mind, body, and spirit normally lead to swing and shot-making prob-lems. That's exactly what happened to Tiger. He blocked tee shots well right of the fairway, hit short-iron approach shots into trouble, usually landing the ball to the side of the green, and also missed some short putts.

What made matters worse was that, after losing the U.S. Open, Tiger compounded his mistakes by working harder to prepare for the British Open. And after losing the British Open, he overprepared for the PGA. All the time during this search for perfection, his mind and body grew more and more tired.

Being mentally fatigued can surely make you physi-cally fatigued, and vice versa. Either way, the tendency is to lose focus and make simple swing faults that are magnified when you hit the driver, simply because this club carries such a reduced degree of loft and is thus less forgiving. In Tiger's case, he had problems off the tee, but, again, he also had problems with the short irons and putter.

Tiger admitted to the golf press that his swing was out of sync. Normally, the tempo or speed of his swing is quite quick, yet it flows rhythmically because the movement of the club is perfectly in sync with the movement of the body. During the 2001 U.S. Open, British Open, and PGA, Tiger simply swung too fast and thus lost control of his shots. When you lose control of your driving and iron games, your putting game usually goes out the window, particularly in high-pressure situations. The tendency is to push putts, as Tiger did many times during the aforementioned majors.

Regardless of Tiger's poor play, by his standards anyway, he did not get down on himself. Like a true champion, Tiger drew strength from his disappointments, knowing he had experienced these same problems before and corrected them. That's the secret to improved play: staying positive in the face of adversity and knowing you can recover your lost game by first getting some rest, then recalling proven mental buzz phrases and working on practice drills. Driving, short-iron play, and putting make up the guts of the game. So if you want to play your best golf, learn how to correct the following common problems, relative to driving, short irons, and putting, just as Tiger did.

TIGER'S TEE SHOT PROBLEMS AND MIND-GAME SOLUTIONS

Off the tee, Tiger hit shots into trouble right of the fairway. Most of the time, he missed the fairway by only inches. However, in major championships you can't afford to do that, because the rough is penalizing. Other times, Tiger landed in deep trouble farther away from the "short grass." Consequently, he paid a price. Instead of being able to attack the flag, he often had to be defensive, advancing a short-iron shot down the fairway only a short distance or playing out sideways.

In analyzing Tiger's blocked shot, I determined that he was picking up the club too abruptly on the backswing, and this fault caused him to cup his left wrist. When there's an indentation or faulty cup in the wrist area, the club tends to point right of target or across the target line at the top of the swing, instead of directly at the target. When you "cross the line," as teachers call it, the clubface opens.

Throughout history, golfers such as Bobby Jones and John Daly have proven that crossing the line at the top of the swing is okay. However, the majority of professionals do not swing the club in this fashion, knowing that their hands aren't educated enough to manipulate the club back on the correct path and plane during the downswing. The irony is that Tiger is talented enough to swing the club this way. Since he first took lessons from Anselmo, however, Tiger was taught that you stand the best chance of delivering the clubface squarely into the ball at impact and hitting your target if the following occur at the top of the swing:

1. The left wrist is flat and lined up with the left forearm.
2. The clubface is square.
3. The clubshaft is parallel to the target line.
4. The clubhead points directly at the target.

During the final three major championships of 2001 that followed Tiger's superb winning play in the Masters, he proved that it's one thing to know what's right, but it's another thing to do what's right. I say this because on several occasions Tiger's club crossed the line at the top, with the clubface finishing open. As Tiger knows, when this happens you will most assuredly come into impact with the clubface open, unless you can manipulate the club back to a square position with your hands.

Ideally, you should be seeking width to the backswing by extending the club away from the target. The secret to accomplishing this goal, and hitting powerfully accurate drives, is letting the big muscles of the body control this action. As renowned golf instructor Phil Ritson explained to me, there are more nerve endings or "frequencies" in your smaller muscles than in your larger muscle groups. This means that if you rely on your hands and wrists to control the backswing, which was Tiger's mistake, it is unlikely that you will move the clubhead on the correct path and plane consistently. You also don't achieve nearly the windup with the hands-orientated backswing as you do when relying on the bigger and stronger muscles of the arms and shoulders. You will swing the club into the ideal slot at the top of the backswing and develop maximum power if you turn the shoulders on a flatter plane than the arms and coordinate this movement with the turning action of the hips.

Many amateurs, in a vain attempt to put more power

into their shot, go to the wrong source. Instead of increasing their body turn, they lift the club straight up into the air with their arms near the completion of the backswing. The right elbow then flies away from the body, pointing outward rather than pretty much directly down to the ground. This faulty right elbow position exaggerates the cup in the left wrist. In turn, the clubshaft points across the target line at the top of the backswing.

MENTAL BUZZ PHRASE: *"Point the club at the target."* Thinking about these words of John Anselmo's when setting up to the ball will promote a good arms-club extension in the takeaway, allow you to match the parallel position at the top, and keep the left wrist flat, the right elbow pointing down, and the clubface square. The result: square clubface-to-ball contact at impact and solid, on-target shots.

Here's a physical drill to complement the mental tip of Anselmo's: Practice swinging the club with your right hand only; this drill will force you to set the club correctly at the top.

TIGER'S SHORT-IRON APPROACH SHOT PROBLEMS AND MIND-GAME SOLUTIONS

When hitting short-iron approach shots into the green, Tiger played a form of "army golf." He hit some shots left of the green and other shots right of target and short of the green. When you consider that Tiger's short-iron shots usually land a few feet to the left or right side of the hole, his off-line play shocked him and his fans. Like his problem off the tee, these bad shots can be traced to some basic faults and cured by thinking of a mental buzz phrase.

In analyzing Tiger's short-iron pull-and-push problems, I noticed that his swing was out of sync due to problems involving hip action on the downswing. Tiger set up squarely to the ball, made an even takeaway action, and correctly shifted his weight over to his right foot and leg on the backswing. But, on the downswing, Tiger drove his legs outward vigorously, to the right of target, and thus prevented his hips from squaring up in the hitting area, then clearing through impact.

To reiterate a point I made earlier, the hips must clear in the downswing to open up a passageway for the arms and hands to swing the club freely into impact with the clubface square to the target. Tiger was taught this swing basic when he was a youngster but struggled to do the right thing during the final three majors of the 2001 professional golf season.

When you drive the legs and hips outward at the start of the downswing, as Tiger did, the arms and hands become blocked by the body, causing the clubface to finish open to the target at impact. The result: a push shot hit right of target.

What's so ironic and crazy about this game is that when you sense a block shot coming, you tend to overrotate the right hand and forearm in a desperate attempt to square up the clubface. This explains why Tiger also pulled some short-iron shots. When the right hand takes over, the left hand collapses and is unable to hold the club squarely to the target. The result of this exaggerated right-hand control: The clubface closes, causing the ball to fly left of target.

MENTAL BUZZ PHRASE: *"Slide, then turn."* Thinking of this phrase, repeated over and over by Butch Harmon, will help promote the correct downswing moves. However, to fully ensure that the clubface finishes in a square impact position, get it into your head that, once arriving at the top of the swing, you must do the following:

1. Shift your weight onto your left foot and leg, so that your hips slide laterally toward the target in a smooth

fashion and, in turn, cause your right arm to drop down close to your side and the club to fall into the ideal hitting slot automatically.

2. Rotate your left hip counterclockwise to give your arms and hands room to freely release the club through the ball.

Should the aforementioned mental buzz phrase not work for you or you need further help in curing your out-of-sync swing, I recommend that you practice one of the following drills taught to me by Harmon:

1. Swing at 75 percent of your normal swing speed.

2. Make a conscious effort to make your back and down speeds identical.

3. Hum a tune before you swing to relieve mental pressure.

PUTTING PROBLEMS AND MIND-GAME SOLUTIONS

Tiger pushed short putts right of target during the 2001 U.S. Open, British Open, and PGA because he fell victim to a fault that's common among club-level amateur players. He played the ball too far back in the stance and swung the putter back inside the target line instead of straight back. The combination of these two faults causes the clubface to open up at impact, with the ball being hit right of the hole.

Phil Mickelson has been working on curing this same problem, but he is having trouble revamping his stroke because he has swung the putter on an exaggerated inside-to-inside path since he was a young boy. He got away with it for a long time because of superb hand-eye coordination and excellent feel in the hands. However, he's since come to realize it is not the most pressure-proof stroke to use in a major championship.

Tiger, on the other hand, has won tournaments as an amateur and as a pro using a straight back-and-through stroke. So, this swing path fault just happened to sneak into his stroke without his realizing it. Letting the ball drift back in his stance didn't help his problem—that's for sure.

MENTAL BUZZ WORDS: *"Straight back and through."* Thinking about this mental buzz phrase before you trigger the putting stroke, and playing the ball opposite your left heel, will better enable you to swing the putter along the target line on the backswing and downswing. Now you will do a good job of "rolling the rock," as Tiger says.

If a friend spots you swinging the putter too far inside the target line or you see yourself doing this on video, you know which words can cure your problem. And if for some reason these words fail to work magic, practice swinging the putter through a gap, between two tees stuck in the green, just as Tiger's father used to have him do.

NOW THAT YOU HAVE LEARNED HOW VITALLY IMportant the mental side of golf is, be smart and devise a program for yourself that helps induce a sense of confidence. Each and every one of us is different, so what works for one golfer may not work for another. For you, maybe building a swing based on the fundamentals and practicing hard to groove various swing elements might be your secret to developing a positive frame of mind. Another golfer could find that a regular routine composed of yoga, exercise, and a healthful diet proves to be the secret to success. While others searching to improve their mental game will find that meditation, or maybe even hypnosis, is the link to mental clarity and freedom from negative thoughts that play havoc with one's ability to swing consistently well, hit on-target shots, and shoot good scores.

The advantage that you now have over other golfers is a headstart in accomplishing your goal. You have learned what golf's greatest player did and still does to think his way to lower scores. Thank you, Tiger Woods, for setting such a fine example and showing us all the road to mental freedom and positive thinking.

◯ THINK LIKE TIGER

• If you are blocking tee shots to the right of the fairway, concentrate on pointing the club at the target when reaching the top of the swing.

• If your problem is pushing short irons, concentrate on shifting your hips laterally toward the target at the start of the downswing, then rotating them counterclockwise in the impact zone.

• If you push putts, play the ball opposite your left heel, then concentrate on swinging the putter straight back and through along the target line.

• Develop your own system for inducing a sense of self-confidence, based on the example set by Tiger Woods.

AFTERWORD

O N SUNDAY, AUGUST 25, 2001, TIGER WOODS
was in the final pairing with Jim Furyk, the leader by
two going into the fourth and final round of the World
Golf Championship NEC Invitational, contested at the
Firestone Country Club in Akron, Ohio.

This was Tiger's first championship since the PGA,
played two weeks earlier. Well rested, mentally focused,
and superconfident about a revamped swing and a practice
tune-up with coach Butch Harmon, Tiger had shot three
previous solid rounds of 66, 67, and 66. Friends, family, fellow pros who know what Tiger does for the game and tel-

evision ratings, and the press who love writing about him wanted to scream out loud, "Tiger is back!" following his frustrating summer. But they realized they were getting ahead of themselves. There was still one more round to play, and, besides, Tiger had to catch Furyk.

Catch up he did, shooting a 69 to Furyk's 71 on day four. However, to regain his superstar status and be officially crowned the world champion of golf, Tiger would need to win a playoff with this very tough and experienced competitor. The two golfing gladiators would start the playoff on hole eighteen and then, if still tied, play seventeen. They would continue until one outdid the other by at least a single stroke.

On the first playoff hole, Tiger looked like a sure winner after Furyk left his third shot in the bunker and faced a forty-foot shot to a pin situated at the base of a slope. When Tiger putted his third shot up to three feet away from the hole, it looked as though he would make par four and Furyk a bogey five at best. How wrong everybody was. Once Furyk shocked everyone by holing out for par, Tiger had to make that three-footer just to tie and keep the playoff alive.

Tiger is the only player I know who can keep his cool in this kind of situation. First of all, he did not panic when Furyk knocked his bunker shot in the hole. Tiger's one of those players who has been trained to expect the other player to hit a miracle shot. That way, if he does, Tiger is better prepared to deal with it mentally. And prepared he was. Tiger stood up to that three-foot pressure putt and knocked it right in the center of the cup.

On the second hole of the playoff, there was even more drama. In fact, Tiger was up against the wall looking like a sure loser. He had to sink a twenty-five-foot uphill, right-to-left-breaking putt to keep his chances for victory alive. Instead of panicking, rushing his prestroke routine, and making a tense, faulty putting stroke, Tiger stayed calm, took his time reading the green, and made a practice stroke with his right hand only (something new for Tiger) to help him feel the distance. Employing one of the smoothest strokes I have ever seen any golfer make under pressure, Tiger then hit the putt. The ball rose up the gentle slope in the green, turned left slightly as it neared the hole, then rolled over the edge. With that par-saving putt, Tiger shocked CBS announcer Ken Venturi who could only say: "I thought I had seen it all." The crowd of fans, experiencing a delayed shock reaction, went wild, with some giving Tiger thunderous applause and others crying out loud: "You Da Man!" As for Tiger, he now had momentum, or what he calls the "Big Mo," on his side.

As if that were not enough tension for the final day of a world championship, there was more on the third hole of the playoff—much more. After hitting his drive into the trees, Tiger smartly punched the ball back to the fairway short of the green, setting up a pitch for his third shot. Furyk had already hit the green in two shots, and his ball came to rest fifteen feet from the hole.

Tiger hit a brilliant pitch to within four feet that must have shook Furyk, for he missed his birdie. Tiger then stood up and sank another solid par putt for par. Yet again, the hole ended in a tie. However, the show was far from over.

On the fourth playoff hole, Tiger made a very good two-putt from thirty-five feet to save par and a tie.

On the fifth playoff hole, Tiger hit an excellent chip, then holed another pressure putt to secure a tie.

On the sixth playoff hole, Tiger hit a super lag putt from sixty feet, scored par, and tied again.

On the seventh hole, Tiger hit a rocket fade drive, then a spinning wedge shot to two feet, then tapped the putt in for a birdie. Victory! Tiger had reentered the winner's circle, but, as he said afterward, "It was a war out there." Indeed it was, but because of his mental toughness, he came out on top.

There you have it—a magnificent playoff battle, a super championship, and the most worthy of world champions. There is no pro golfer as resilient as Tiger Woods. Granted, there are other fine players on the world tour. But make no mistake: Tiger is the only player who possesses the "it" quality that allows him, under the greatest of pressure, to pull off a Bobby Thomson–type feat or, as his friend Michael Jordan used to do: make the winning shot at the buzzer. Tiger proved, once again, that he has the "right stuff," by winning both the 2002 Masters and U.S. Open championships.

Here's hoping that Tiger stays around for a long time to come. He's the best thing that ever happened to golf.

ACKNOWLEDGMENTS

I THANK LITERARY AGENT GILES ANDERSON, OF THE Scott Waxman Agency, and editor Jennifer Repo, of the publishing house Penguin Putnam, for believing in my idea to write a book analyzing the mental game of Tiger Woods. I am indebted to Putnam's editorial and promotional staff for getting behind *Think Like Tiger* and making valuable suggestions.

I'm also grateful to Earl Woods, Tiger's father, for answering questions I had relating to things he and his wife Tida taught Tiger to help him enhance the mental side of his game.

Further gratitude is owed to Tiger's former coach John Anselmo, and not only for providing information directly related to the development of Tiger's mental game prowess and writing the foreword to the book you now hold in your hands. Additionally, he acted on my behalf as a messenger, putting forth to Tida Woods some questions I had relating to the role she played in introducing her son to Buddhism and meditation. I had requested Mrs. Woods' telephone number from Anselmo, so that I could question her directly. But he explained to me that she is a very private person and that it would be better if he told her about the book I was writing and interviewed her. I had no problem with that arrangement, knowing that they were close friends and understood each other.

Three other people, Rudy Duran, Dr. Jay Brunza, and Claude "Butch" Harmon, Jr., deserve recognition for helping me better understand how Tiger thinks his way to lower scores. Rudy Duran taught Tiger from the age of four until ten. After one long conversation with Duran, I concluded that he had a positive influence on Tiger in terms of the role the mind plays in golf, particularly with regard to visualizing shots before you play them. Dr. Jay Brunza, a Navy clinical psychologist, hypnotized Tiger and served as his caddy/mentor throughout much of his amateur career. Claude "Butch" Harmon, Jr., Tiger's most recent coach, shared with me the secrets he had learned about the mental game from the great Ben Hogan and had passed on to Tiger.

I thank the top teachers of the PGA of America and the United States Golf Teachers Federation for their opinions on why Tiger is so good mentally. I also appreciate the viewpoints of tour professionals, television golf commentators, and my fellow members of the golf press, most notably Tim Rosaforte, and the information I received from Tiger's former caddy, Michael "Fluff" Cowan.

Special thanks go to Robert Kraut of the booklegger, a golf-related distribution house, for supplying me with videos of the major championships won by Tiger. Because I could replay these tapes over and over, I was able to study Tiger more carefully than when watching him play live at a tournament which I, of course, also have done. This tape-review process allowed me to analyze Tiger's preswing routine, shot-making choices, and strategies. Therefore, even though I was not able to get into his head and read his mind, I was given great insight into his thinking process through his actions.

Last, but certainly not least, I thank California-based golf pro and friend of the Woods family, Ray Oakes, for sharing with me his experience of being hypnotized by Dr. Jay Brunza.

INDEX

K
Koch, Gary, 115

L
Larry King Live, 43
Las Vegas Invitational, 68
Learner, Rich, 6
Left-to-right fade, 17
Leonard, Sugar Ray, 55–56
Lerner, Rich, 47
Long putt, 19
Looking Glass Drill, 58–59
Los Alamitos Golf Course (Cypress,
    Calif.), 23
Low Short-Iron Spinner, 113–14
Lyle, Sandy, 101

M
McLean, Jim, 93
Maiden, Stewart, 26
Maltby, Roger, 115
Masters, 77, 104, 113, 116
May, Bob, 121
Meadowlark Golf Course (Huntington
    Beach, Calif.), 23
Medicine Ball Exercise, 52–53
Medinah Country Club (Medinah, Ill.), 107
Meditation, 61–64, 93
Medium Iron Stop-Shot, 110–11
Medium putt, 18
Mental challenges, 125–43
Mental connection, 14
Mental fatigue, 127
Mental images, 24–25, 101–3, 124
    Fairway Bunker Cut, 111–13
    Low Short-Iron Spinner, 113–14
    Medium Iron Stop-Shot, 110–11
    Rocket Fade, 106–8
    Sand Splash, 115–16